Sales Tales

Sales Tales

James P. Shannon

Writers Club Press
San Jose New York Lincoln Shanghai

Sales Tales

Writers Club Press
an imprint of iUniverse.com, Inc.

For information address:
iUniverse.com, Inc.
5220 S 16th, Ste. 200
Lincoln, NE 68512
www.iuniverse.com

ISBN: 0-595-18152-X

Printed in the United States of America

PREFACE

Sales Tales is a collection of anecdotes that occurred to a father and his two sons over a seventy-year time span. The work has two goals. The first is to reveal to a new sales recruit an overview of some successes and failures that might happen in a sales career. The second goal is to assist individuals to understand what a spouse, sibling, or friend might be experiencing in his or her daily work as a salesman.

It is an easy read. It is a fun read. It is worth your time.

INTRODUCTION

Sales Tales is a collection of stories and advice pertinent to the selling profession. Almost all of these tales happened to the members of our family starting with our dad whose sales career spanned the years from 1910 to 1945. Following in his footsteps, his sons sold from 1945 to 1980. Examples from both generations are included. There are also stories about salespeople who were not part of our family but were employed by the same corporation or industry as the family members. Most of these accounts are short and can be told on a single page.

In addition to stories about various sales experiences, these pages contain truisms about interpersonal relationship in the workplace that are as valid today as they were in the early years of our family members' sales' histories.

The highway of life is filled with chuckholes and detours. An old religious proverb states:

"God gives catastrophes and problems to those He loves." A salesman can't help pleading, "Please, God, don't love sales people so much."

CONTENTS

Salesmanship

SALESMANSHIP

Applying for a Sales Job

When a salesman applies for a job, he is bombarded with conflicting directions and advice. Some large corporations use their own personnel department for recruiting and interviewing salespeople. Other organizations use employment agencies; still others have their own sales departments that insist on complete control of the hiring of new salesmen and run blind ads. The variables are endless.

Interviews continue this wide pattern. Some companies studiously project a friendly, compassionate, kindly atmosphere. A meeting in a company like this can be pleasant, warm and enjoyable. Other companies will be 100 percent opposite. A growling, miserable, antagonistic person will pick and prod. Unpleasant prying questions will be hurled at the sales applicant. At times, an experienced, well-educated salesman will find himself sputtering and flustered.

It is a fact that an applicant for a particular job should do his level best to have the interviewer recognize all his assets. At the same time, in the back of his mind, the candidate should be interviewing the company.

CAN I WORK FOR THIS COMPANY?

1. Company rules—too restrictive?
2. The company executive—too abrasive?
3. The company product and image—excellent?
4. Is growth in the company possible?

Looking Before You Leap

When the Russians sent their dog *Sputnik* around the moon, our federal government took immediate action to improve the teaching of math and science in all our schools.

The Singer Corporation had an educational filmstrip division in Chicago named S.V.E. with huge sums of money pouring out of Washington to improve our schools. Naturally S.V.E. rushed to enlarge their sales staff. A very experience and knowledgeable salesman was interviewed. He flew up from Baton Rouge, Louisiana, met all the key people, passed all the personal interviews and was accepted. The S.V.E. sales manager had attended college in Louisiana, and to be friendly, he invited the new recruit home for dinner. First thing the next morning the new man announced, "I quit." The stunned sales training manager asked, "Why?"

"Last night I went to the sales manager's house for dinner. I discovered he has worked here for 20 years. Back in Louisiana my garage is better than his house. No sense in starting, much less staying." He left. A salesman must decide: *Can I survive? Can I make a good living? Does this company allow its employees to do well?* When you take the new sales position, you absolutely should know those answers.

Following Rules of the Resume

As a tool to sell oneself, the resume, online or in soft copy, can be an invaluable tool. Do companies necessarily hire employees on the basis of what they have stipulated as the training and experiences that should be reflected in the resume? This story is a classic example of a hiring fluke.

Abbott Laboratories of North Chicago is a Goliath among giants. It is a well-managed company, and unlike other large corporations, it has stayed in one field— medical care.

About twenty years ago, Abbot's Research and Development Division produced new equipment that could be used in intensive care rooms of hospitals worldwide. Initially, ten new sales people with science backgrounds were needed to sell the intensive care equipment. The company placed an ad in the *Chicago Tribune* asking for people with just such background to apply. After a period of ninety days, only four people with the science qualifications had responded to the ad. What to do? The company devised a plan to hire ten people for a ninety-day period and train them in-house. At the end of the science training, all of them would be tested and those who graded highest would be hired permanently.

A recent Princeton graduate was working in a lumberyard part-time while he hunted for a job. His family saw Abbott's ad in the *Chicago Tribune.* They encouraged their son to apply. Princeton had given him a degree in Social Studies. He had not taken a single science course. Under pressure, he finally mailed his resume to Abbott. One of the secretaries in the Personnel

Department who saw the resume remarked, "My boyfriend attended Princeton and to graduate he had to study."

The right person heard the secretary's remarks and the Princeton graduate was told to come in for the ninety days of training. In the posttest, he placed third and was hired. Later Abbott's personnel office told him that his resume was a disaster. It broke all the rules; it was too long, too personal did not match the specific details that Abbott considered necessary

This story is not meant to downplay the importance of a well-written resume, but to underscore the fact that candidates for a job must never give up on possible job leads.

Selling as an Art Form

There are hundreds if not thousands of *selling* jobs that can be dull, drab, almost soul killing in their monotony. Retail sales, in particular, can be completely boring if a salesman or saleswoman permits it to happen. But there are those individuals whose bright smile and quick wit can say or do the proper action to make that sale a success for both the buyer and the seller.

Years ago on Chicago's state street at the O'Connor and Goldberg shoe store, one of their sales people made over $100 thousand in commissions selling shoes. His sales were made by appointment. The salesman maintained a file of customer names, phone numbers, shoe size, and individual tastes. When new shipments arrived, the prospect would be phoned and an appointment set. Each customer felt his or her time would not be wasted. Both seller and buyer were happy. The salesman did recognize the individual likes and dislikes of each person.

This example is a classic one of how selling can be an art form. Unique thinking, special programming, the correct and proper attitude and approach can make selling both a joyful and a fulfilling experience.

The keys to each sales problem are as many as the pebbles of the California shoreline. It does take an individual who has the proper attitude and imagination to put together the right keys to unlock a successful career in selling.

Learning When to Stop Talking

Few people remember when our railroads used kerosene lamps, lanterns and signals. When our country electrified its cities, the electrification of the railroads became an immediate need. It is quite easy to imagine the fantastic costs involved. Every rail car needed new fixtures along with the necessary batteries, transformers and generators. Miles and miles of wiring were strung to activate switches, crossing lights, barricades and gates.

The size of each rail system and the number of cars involved, forced some of these railroad companies to spend tens of millions of dollars. This was in an era when the average man labored for one dollar a day. It took a few years before every rail line completed electrification. The old L&N Rail Road (Louisville & Nashville) did not modernize. The president of this line was super conservative and fought off any and all new developments. He firmly believed that electricity was dangerous; just a fad. His thinking was typically horse and wagon in every way.

Because the L&N did not electrify, the pressures from customers and employees began to build. The president finally relented and called in the Western Railway Supply to get estimates on materials and labor. The salesman involved returned with a complete schedule and contract. The total contract was just over $10 million. His commission was 2 percent. He would earn over $200 thousand. The president deliberated long, asked many specific questions and finally signed the contract.

Naturally, the salesman thanked him profusely, then he said, "Do you mind if I ask a question?"

The L&N president said, "No, I don't mind. Go ahead."

"Why did you wait so long to electrify?" The president said, "What did you say?" The salesman repeated his question.

"Let me see that contract." The president said. When he got it in his hands he tore it up. His words, "I guess I'll wait another year or two to electrify," and that's what he did.

When the sale is made SHUT UP!

Knowing the Facts

Advertising, creativity, and consistency do a highly effective job of influencing our buying habits. It can actually take a weakness of a particular product and use that as a selling feature. General Tire constantly fostered and drove home the concept of quality. Some ads showed a huge derrick lifting a railroad locomotive up into the air. Cables were fastened to four General Squeegee tires, and they in turn were attached to cables that were tied to the locomotive. What that had to do with the general tire strength, who knows? But that was the ad.

At all sales training sessions the quality, the strength of all General Tire products was accented over and over. When you take a slow studied look at advertising and sales training you see a form of hypnotism, a form of brain washing pounded into the salesmen's psyche. One Chicago General Tire salesman believed that quality story so fully, so completely that he actually believed anyone he knew was in danger of losing his life he drove a car that used any other tire.

While at the factory in Akron, he was escorted with a group to observe the actual manufacturing and production of the General Tire line. As the group was escorted through the plant, he noticed brand names he considered inferior: Atlas, Ajax, India, Diamond, all off brand tires sold in chain store operations. The tires were considered second-rate. When the tour guide was questioned as to where was the difference between General Tire's specifications and the off brand tires, he was assured there was a difference. Eventually he discovered an answer he didn't want to hear or see.

- Dupont made all the tire fabric.
- The United States Government controlled the rubber content.
- The steel beads came from U.S. Steel.
- The tire molds were made by a McNeil company and were identical for all tire companies.
- One union, the Alcohol workers Union of the U.S. controlled the manpower at every tire company.
- The difference? The brand name that was molded on the sidewall when the tire was cured constituted the only difference.

VIVA LA DIFFERENCE!

There are times when it is better not to know.

Reporting Sales

When a salesman is hired to sell a product or service, the recruit assumes if he is successful at selling, his job will be secure! Not so! The paper work becomes almost as important as selling, sometimes even more so. There are sales managers who insist on typed reports. Some sat that reports must be mailed by Friday P.M., not Saturday A.M.

Expense reports are another sore point with some. Each item listed must have a receipt. One salesman found his company deducting $1.37 from his weekly expense report because of lack of a receipt. To retaliate, he turned in a phony $5.00 receipt the following week. To do that he bought all his gas at a $5.00 total each time. It annoyed management, but they let it happen.

When a company has almost one hundred men out in the territories, it doesn't take too much imagination to recognize it is almost impossible for a manager to find the time to read each and every report thoroughly. Believing that much of their work was never read, some men use *colors* instead of the names for men they called on. There are plenty of color names, White, Black, Brown, all across this country. Salesmen named customers *colors:* Orange, Purple, Yellow, Fuchsia, and Amber.

After a while one man grew tired with the *color* game and decided for fun to switch to the names of *animals*: Fox, Lion, Bear, Katz. One day the salesman listed a Mr. Hippopotamus and was called in on that one. He explained to the sales manager that he had used that name just to see if his reports were actually being read. The managers bought it! They do read some reports.

Learning Company Rules

When salesmen join a new company, the smart ones, maybe they should be described as the shrewd ones, ask the experienced salesmen on the staff for the basic rules or company sales policies. If a new salesman is open, guileless, and no threat to the staff, the team may tell him there aren't many rules to remember. In the 1950's, the drill may have gone something like this:

1. Make six calls per day: three calls in the morning and three in the afternoon.

2. Keep your expense account under $100 per week.

3. Try to write one order per day.

One new salesman moved to his territory and did his best to follow the rules. If he hustled, he could make five or six calls each morning, and again five or six calls each afternoon. When he did that, his three days of hustling accounted for a five-day week or a total of thirty calls. By hustling, it cost him more than $100 in expenses, so by not working Monday or Friday, he was able to keep his expense account under $100. The other rule, five orders per week, was a bit more difficult. One of the older salesmen had quite by accident remarked, "I always ask my customers to send the orders to my house" This was not company policy but was valuable knowledge for the new salesman. There would be days when two, three, or four orders would come to his home. Each day by sending in one, or at times two, he would keep the rules. The home office was happy and so was the sales rep.

Rules are rules, but some must be interpreted loosely in order for a salesman to survive.

Compensation

COMPENSATION

This chapter will illustrate types of conflicts between management and the sales people they hire. Corporate thinkers find it difficult to appreciate, much less reward a salesperson.

Most corporations list selling costs under expenses. To improve profits, managers carefully supervise, curtail, and completely ignore the adage, "Until someone sells something, nothing happens."

Successful salesmen sometimes have a positive outlook by reason of their genes. Upon joining a new company, salesmen often see in their mind a golden sunrise, a bright day coming, a rewarding future on the horizon. If they did not see that uplifting pleasant scene, they wouldn't take the job. That blinding light in their face at times prevents them from inquiring about exactly what the salary, bonuses, and perks will be. Some organizations have a pay plan so confusing so complicated it would take a legal genius to understand the fine print.

Warning:

Before you take the job, be sure to understand what your total income should be.

A Ridiculous Commission

Back in the mid 1950s, General Tire had only 2 percent of the Chicago market. National surveys projected they should have a 10-12 percent share of the market. The Interstate General Tire Franchise was organized to improve that picture. A member of the franchise had personal connections to the local Mafia. The OK Truck Line was rumored to have a manager in the Mafia. All beer brewed in Milwaukee was shipped to Chicago via the OK Truck Line. This was a fact of life in Chicago and that practice existed when beer came back after Prohibition in 1934. Phone calls were made and a sales meeting was set. The salesman met the manager at his huge mansion in River Forest Illinois. The main living room had a two-story, cathedral ceiling. The floor space held a half-dozen sofas and countless end tables. It was grand and plush, but the atmosphere intimidated the salesman. Very graciously, the manager of the OK Truck Line agreed to order General Tries for his new fleet of 200 trailers. Each trailer had eight 1000x 20 tires and tubes, amounting to 1,600 tires and tubes for the fleet.

This volume cost was approximately $160 thousand. The Mafia leader told our salesman there was only one requirement. The General Tire price must equal the going rate. Fair enough. The salesman did not realize how cautious and clever Mafia businessmen can be. The tire industry recognizes O.E.M.(Original Equipment Manufacturer). OK Truck Line made one trailer each year to qualify for O.E.M. The price was

10 percent below the franchise dealer cost. On bringing the P.O. back to the dealership, in his mind the visualized 5 percent of $160 thousand equals $8 thousand.

Our salesman calculated one percent of $160 thousand equals $16 hundred; but the parent company in Akron paid him one-tenth of one percent on $160 thousand, or $160.00. Our salesman said, " Stick it."

Akron did. Just one more example of a salesman not checking in advance to determine exactly what the compensation should be.

A Compensation Problem

The inconsistencies in income within the same company between men in two different regions can be unbelievably different. At one time, personal circumstances of a salesman in North Carolina and another in Ohio created monstrous differences.

Singer Corporation, producing audiovisual equipment for schools, employed a Southern region salesman with a small family and a wife who was a high school principal. He owned his home, had two cars and was in excellent financial condition. He was hired at a 25 percent commission and paid his own expenses. The Midwest man had a big family; seven children with two in college. His wife did not work. They had one car and rented a house. They weren't poor, but he needed a steady income and an adequate expense account.

Due to an increase of federal funds for schools, audiovisual educational materials were in high demand. The total market volume soared. Salesmen topped records monthly. The Home Office couldn't have been more pleased to receive 400,000+sales volume from North Carolina and 600,000 from Ohio. These totals pinpoint the problem with compensation.

The North Carolina man received $100,000; that is 25 percent commission.

The Ohio man received $19,400.

Salary	$10,000.00
Car	1,800.00
Expenses	5,100.00
Bonus	2,500.00
	$ 19,400.00

The Ohio man sold $200 thousand more than the North Carolina man.

The Ohio salesman's income was $80,600 less than the North Carolina salesman. Compensation? What does it mean?

Another Compensation Problem

Shortly after World War II, an ex B-24 pilot started working for DeMert and Dougherty. This company sold marine supplies, including turpentine, linseed oil, paint thinners, and industrial alcohol. In the winter, the salesman called on gas station owners, in addition to paint and hardware store managers. Prestone for car radiator systems was an absolute necessity in the north. The product Heet, a form of industrial alcohol called anhydrous alcohol, was water free and when added to the gasoline tank, it mixed with the water that came from condensation and could be burned in the car's engine. It helped prevent gas line freeze ups.

Chicago winters can be severe. Trying to start a cold engine can be a problem and there are days when it's impossible. Heet sold well in Chicago. The ex B-24 pilot-turned-salesman was both eager and aggressive. He called on paint and hardware stores, as well as gas stations from 47th to 95th Streets, from the Lake west to the Chicago city limits. No way could he get rich selling Heet, yet he worked hard and made good bonuses. He was pleased with the salary.

After a year, the president of the company called the salesman into his office and asked if he would like to take a long trip through Minnesota and North and South Dakota. The Reinhart Brothers Company had seventy-five salesmen traveling through the Dakotas, Montana, Wyoming, all the way to Oregon and Washington. Being young and eager to have the chance to travel, the salesman jumped at the opportunity.

First, he took the Chicago Northwestern Railroad to Minneapolis. There he had mild success. Then on to North Dakota by Greyhound Bus to Fargo and the Reinhart Brothers Store. At Reinhart's he met a big Swede, Vic—6'4" and over 280 pounds. He didn't smile, talked little, but mostly just sat and stared. Our salesman's pitch took only three or four minutes. He even had a small record player to let the prospective customer listen to a spot radio message about Heet recorded for local stations about Heet. He gave a sample bottle of the product and a price-list sheet, showing dealer, wholesaler, and freight car discounts. The sales materials didn't take up much room on Vic's desk. The salesman asked Vic for the order and sat there and waited! He was taught that a salesman should ask for the order and then wait. If you don't wait, you might lose.

Vic sat stone-faced. Finally, he said, "Do you know what I'm waiting for?"

Our salesman said, "No, I don't."

Then Vic said "I'm was waiting for pressure, and if you gave me any I was going to pick you up and throw your ass out into the street. You are the third person Demert Dougherty sent up here. The others were two Chicago high-pressure bozos. One even had the gall to put a pen in my hand and asked me to sign the order. Is Heet any good? Will it sell?"

The salesman's answer was both honest and sincere. "I have three children. I make my winter income selling Heet to Chicago gas stations."

Vic dared him to sell Heet in Fargo and had a local salesman drive him around. They returned with three orders out of the five calls that they made. It was a guaranteed sale. If Heet did-n't sell, it could be returned for full credit. Vic set up an order and scheduled two carloads a month for November, December and January. Our salesman was accustomed to selling one or two cases at a time. This 3,600 case order overwhelmed him. The total order was worth almost $100 thousand.

Making $2.00 per case in Chicago, the salesman knew that DeMert would not pay that much commission. Being fair, he realized that a $7,200 commission was impossible. On the Greyhound bus back to Minneapolis and later on the N.W. Railroad back to Chicago, he dropped his expectations to a commission of 50 cents a case. That was still $1,800. When the salesman handed the president of DeMert the order for 3,600 cases, his face almost broke from the huge grin of joy. The new recruit asked what commission he would get from this order. He believed in the fairness of the system and expected to get just treatment. He was shocked to the point of stunned disbelief.

The president said, "Fargo North Dakota is not your terri-tory. Your territory is the south side of Chicago. You will not get a commission."

The young salesman never did get a cent for his effort. In a month or two he moved on, a bit wiser, but not richer.

The Moral: Before beginning any job, special program, or sales effort, both parties should have a complete understand-ing of what the compensation will be, preferably in writing.

Quotas Should Not Be Easy?

After reading the previous examples about the life of a salesman, we discover it is not an easy one. Security has a meaning in some occupations, but it is meaningless in sales. Salesmen have no union, never have, and never will. Each man is on his own. No matter how capable he might be, a single salesman alone wields no strength.

One year a Singer division was in a fast growing market. It was in the educational field and the Federal government was pouring funds in to improve education. We, as a nation, have always believed that money can buy anything. Money can improve a situation; money can change a situation, but it just isn't so. Educational funds must have purpose and direction to improve our schools.

Federal funds for audiovisual equipment poured into Singer. All 80 salesmen beat their quotas by 100 percent or more. The company grew from $7 million dollars to $16 million in one year. The sales volume in some states doubled and some tripled. The funds forwarded in the parent conglomerate were astounding. It was a bonanza year!

As the national sales manager set sales goals and quotas for the coming year, he thought the figures he outlined were realistic and optimistic. He had no way of forecasting what did take place. At the Singer conglomerate headquarters, the MBAs were furious at the size of individual bonuses. They had to take action to correct the error. Action came swiftly.

They fired the national sales manager.
Giant corporations can be confusing.

The Salary was Different

The dictionary's #1 definition for compensation tells us it means to be equivalent; to make up; to pay; to remunerate. In a business context, compensation is easy to understand and quite easy to accomplish. But the man or company doing the hiring, tries to employ a person for the least number of dollars and perks he can. Because of that mindset, misunderstandings and misinterpretations take place.

For over a two-year period, a manufacturing agent representing a wide range of sources, called faithfully on an educational materials corporation. The treasurer of the company was also the purchasing agent. The company's needs were varied, and the ordering volume of a particular invoice item could be as many as 100 thousand or as small as a single desk or chair. To search out sources for these wide-ranging needs could be severely time consuming. The treasurer and the manufacturing agent were both born and reared in Chicago. The two developed an easy cordial relationship and all went well.

The president of the education company was a "hands on" CEO and when technicians decided to develop a new technique of picture story study prints, the initial product volume would be in the 50,00 range. There was not only a special printing technique for the cards, but they had to be stored and assembled before being gathered into vinyl envelopes for sales distribution.

The back and forth, give and take of an order this gigantic found the manufacturing agent on the education company's premises almost daily. The president of the manufacturing company admired the tenacity and persistence of the salesman and asked if the agent would consider taking over the state of Ohio.

It so happened that the agent had a wife and seven children in suburban Wheaton.

His wife was constantly nagging him to take a steady job with a steady income. Up until this time, a big-ticket order could bring two or three thousand dollars in income. Then there could be weeks when the take home pay might be $20 or $30. It isn't easy to run a household with such an inconsistent income. The agent's wife told him $200 each and every week would give her the wherewithal to pay all household bills, mortgage, insurance and medicine, actually a very sizable amount for the time.

The agent was hired at $200 per week and the sales manager rode with him to Ohio for the first two weeks. In the middle of the second week, when the salesman called home, his wife told him that he didn't have the salary he thought he would have. The president of the company interpreted the $200 per week as $800 per month or $9600 per year. Then they deducted Blue Cross, Social Security, and Federal Income Tax. The total of $200 shrunk to $178.

The agent and the sales manager returned to the home office that same day.

Sitting with the president and the sales manager to discuss the salary misunderstanding was the ultimate confrontation. It wasn't easy for the salesman to curb his Irish temper, but he did. His words spewed out in a torrent. $200 per week take-home is not $178. His wife needed a minimum of $200. The President rebutted that he found it impossible to believe that a salesman would request a "take-home" amount. But he did want this agent to sell in Ohio. He adjusted the figures.

This is another classic of how compensation can be a problem.

Bonding

BONDING

There are two main types of salespeople: the *numbers* people and the *artists*. When we focus on the subject of bonding, it might seem that the *numbers* sales people are being demeaned. That is not so. There are thousands and thousands of sales people worldwide whose main efforts are on filling up the shelves. They go from store to store, from warehouse to warehouse to see that the flow of products from producer, to stores, to consumers is continuous. All salespeople have the same goal- to see that their product or service flows to the consumer as smoothly and as easily as possible. But there is another category of sales people who do creative selling. Hence the term *artist* seems to describe them. It suggests that the person is a dreamer with an active imagination. He is always willing to attempt new and different techniques. Bonding exists in almost all inter-personal relationships. The more experiences people have in common, the wider the base for a lasting and satisfying relationship. For the buyer, it is both pleasing and satisfying to meet the artist salesman. For the salesman, to have another person recognize his value and appreciate his efforts is equally satisfying. The artist is conscious that it is quite easy to destroy a bond. The list of possibilities is long and treacherous. Some subjects of conversation that are danger zones capable of destroying a bond include politics, religion, and nationalities. A salesman must approach these areas cautiously

A Puppy Can Bind

Eli Lilly, the pharmaceutical company in Indianapolis, Indiana had a national sales force of about a thousand salesmen. A company of this size is a prime customer for an office supply manufacturers that produces loose-leaf ring binders and sales aids.

Eli Lilly's purchasing agent was named Welch. Just before Christmas, the Welch's pet Cocker Spaniel that belonged to his two little girls was hit and killed by a car. Bill Truax, a salesman for the hundred year-old Barrett Binder Co. in Chicago, heard about the accident and immediately bought a registered Cocker Spaniel puppy and drove to Indianapolis to give it to Welches as a gift. That happened on Christmas Eve. Welch and Truax became immediate and long-lasting friends. It wasn't the cost of a pedigreed puppy. It was the sensitive act of responding to the sadness and sorrow of Welch's two little daughters at Christmas time. This kindly act became a *bond* between the two men that grew stronger and tighter as time went by. They were close, good friends. The bond was there.

A rival sales organization in the loose-leaf binder industry sent their new man into Lilly to try to open the door for some business. The salesman called on Welch at Eli Lilly. It was a pleasant interview. Welch told the story of how Truax and he had become close friends. He went on to say all salesmen were welcome, but that Truax would always have the binder business. As was customary, the new salesman's report included the details of the conversation. A smart salesman, a wise salesman appreciates being told that there was little sense wasting sales effort and time on an account that was locked up by the competition.

His immediate boss was VP of sales, a caustic, conceited, abrasive know-it-all who told the new salesman to meet him at the Indianapolis airport. He would demonstrate how to open up the Lilly account. Welch, who was always warm and courteous, received them cordially. After quietly listening to the vice president's sales presentation, he turned to the salesman and asked, "Did you tell your boss what I told you about Truax?"

"Yes, I did," the new salesman responded.

Welch turned to the vice president, "Let me tell you something. If Truax dies or goes out of this business, you and your company would be the last ones I would call." You have wasted my time. Good day!"

When a bond is strong it is impenetrable.

Sour Milk Can Bind

A few companies teach bonding in their sales training sessions; most do not. The salesmen who think of their sales profession as an *art form* believe in it. The *numbers people*, the MBA's and CPA'S, do not. This *bonding* section has an odd twist to it.

A young salesman had an early appointment with the chief purchasing agent (P.A.) of U.S. Steel. Halfway through the presentation, the purchasing agent got up and started to pace around the room. He kept sniffing. He finally said, "Something stinks in this room. I can't figure out what is, but God it's strong and sour, too." He paced and paced. Finally, he was standing next to the young salesman. He said, "Sorry, I don't want to hurt your feelings, but that sour smell is coming from you."

The salesman removed his coat, and there on the back of his vest was a long splash of sour milk. He had burped his newborn son before he came to work that morning. The P.A. laughed, got a wet towel and helped to wash the vest. Naturally, the salesman was highly embarrassed. To put him at ease, the P.A. told about some of the problems he had had with raising his own family. They became close friends because of that sour milk. *Bonding* comes in many forms and odors!

Baseball Can Bind

Quite some time ago when first earning my spurs, I worked alongside my Dad. He had been a salesman all of his life. In fact, at times I believed he must have been in sales in a past existence. He always seemed to come up with the right technique, either to close a sale or to open the door for a new one. One miserable, hot July day, we had called on the McCook Stone Quarry. You could see the white dust everywhere. It was in your nose and eyes, in your mouth and hair. We were headed home and I was glad the day was ending. Dad was driving north on Harlem Avenue in Chicago, and as we approached the Arrow Petroleum yard, he turned in. Irritated, dirty and crabby, I shouted, "Where the hell do you think you're going?"

Dad said, "I've got an idea. It might work on Frank Schreiber. You won't have to do a damned thing. I'll do it all."

Frank Schreiber, who managed the largest fleet of trucks delivering fuel oil in the Chicago area. We had a General Tire dealership, and oil fleets use a lot of tires each year, maybe as much as $50 to $60 thousand in volume in a year. That is a top account. Over a three-year period, we had different salesmen take turns calling on Arrow, but in all that time, no one ever got a sale. Weekly sales reports all had lengthy details about Frank Schreiber. He was always cranky, rude, and unpleasant. He never said hello, never shook hands— a tough, tough customer.

We walked into the office at the end of the yard. It was hot, dusty— flies everywhere. The window was open and hot gusts of fuel oil stench blew in. Schreiber was sitting at his desk. Without looking up he said, "What do you want?"

"Are you busy?" dad asked.

"Yep," answered Schreiber. He continued with his adding machine. We stood in the doorway 10-12 minutes. To me it seemed like a year. Schreiber finally stopped and again. "What do you want?"

Once again my Dad repeated, "Are you busy?"

"Yep," and he went back to the adding machine. Still we stood there. This time it was only for 5-6 minutes. Schreiber finished his task and looked up.

"What do you want and who are you?"

"You're Frank Schreiber, aren't you?" dad said. Without waiting for an answer, Dad went on.

"We wanted to meet the man who runs the best fleet of trucks in Chicago."

I'm not certain if it was the best, but it was a good solid well-run organization. Schreiber was good at his job. One word led to another. Both men were about the same age; both loved baseball. They seemed to have much in common. Raised in Logan Square, both graduated from Crane Technical High School, but not at the same time. Finally, after 20-30 minutes of chatter, we got up to go.

"Aren't you going to tell me who you are and why you came in here?" Schreiber asked in an almost friendly way.

Dad shocked me with his answer. "No, we won't. We will come next week and give you our best sales pitch."

With that we left. It was the damnedest sales presentation I had ever witnessed or read about. When we returned, Schreiber couldn't have been more pleasant. To top it off, we got the account and kept it for over ten years. Schreiber did not change. He still continued to be miserable with all who called on him, but not with us. Baseball can bond.

A.A. Binds

General Tire Corporation owned a Kansas City dealership. According to national ratings, it took a bigger percentage out of that local market than it was entitled to. The manager a slight, polite, well-mannered gentleman was successful and the dealership made money. The office personnel, sales force, and service men all knew their jobs and performed well. Akron was pleased that the Kansas City operation presented no problems, no complaints. All was well. Except for one thing. The percentage of profit wasn't as high as it should have been considering the size or the volume. A team of auditors went in to study the operation, and they were expected to set in place new directives to improve profitability. In just a few days they discovered this highly successful, respected manager had a gigantic drinking problem. As they delved deeper and deeper into sales expenses, they found that the company rented on a yearly basis, the pent house of the Muhlbock Hotel, equipped with an open bar and hot & cold hors d'oeuvres, and a piano player from 6:00 p.m. to 2:00 a.m. Customers were always welcome. The manager spent from noon till 2:00 a.m. seven days a week at the hotel. There were times when he slept there. He did sell tires. His volume was beyond realistic expectations. It took quite a while for the auditors to finally ascertain what the Muhlbock escapade cost in sales expense. Our quiet, respected manager had his bookkeeper issue a check for cartage when actually the check was sent to the Muhlbock

Hotel. The total hotel expenses for two years were more than $250,000.

He was FIRED!

The National Sales Manager, we'll call him Mr. S, headquartered in Akron quickly recognized the talent and the skills of this ex-sales manager. Mr. S. was one of the original six alcoholics recruited to initiate an "AA" program to assist his only son Bob. Mr. S. stepped forward and recruited the ex-Kansas City Manager to join "AA." He put him back on the General Tire payroll at $25,000 per year. All seemed well. But it wasn't!

Quite unexpectedly, the CEO and major stockholder of General Tire, was furious. He wanted a head to roll. Once again, our fantastic Mr. S. had an answer. The Ex's salary was raised to $50,000. One half would be deducted monthly to repay the lost $250,000. The CEO was satisfied. So was Mr. S. Our Ex continued to sell General Tires.

CEOs

CEOs

In studying the History of Western Civilization, we can't help but wonder *how did our almost complete adoration of and submission to power begin?* Was it a result of the phenomenon we know as the Divine Right of Kings? Was it a concept derived from Christianity as an element in "God's Plan?" What is it in our very nature that makes us submissive to leaders?

A leader can be a CEO or a president of a corporation. He or she can be a president of a college, a school board, a hospital, or any local group. We seem prone to cater to the whims and wishes of those in command. We laugh and seem to appreciate the humor in the stories that our leaders tell. Does this attitude from cave days make us turn to a leader to give us direction? We accept, not only willingly, but almost hungrily the idea that another will direct our daily efforts and control our thoughts. The concept of "leadership" seems to be lost. We now want directors and directives. Odd?

Dads of CEOs

Our media constantly bombards us with polls, surveys, and research information. It is never ending. The consumer wonders if the all-invasive computer, coupled with the World Wide Web, is always vigilant to discover tidbits of information that will capture and hold the public's attention.

An information junkie does describe my attitude. Years ago when I spent considerable time calling on Midwest schools, I traveled regularly to Ohio State University. Dr. Edgar Dale was an English Department head, and he was a true joy to hear. If I heard it once, I heard the phrase a thousand times. "The weakest tool in the American classrooms is the teachers voice." Another favorite quote: "Man learns six times more from the eyes than the ears." Some will immediately quote stories about the phenomenal learning power of the deaf, but for any given axioms there are always words of rebuttal.

The classrooms of our nation, including universities, have consistently set up curriculum in one-hour segments knowing full well that educational research conducted by Harvard's School of Education almost 150 years ago disputes the wisdom of that practice.

Here are some statistics from the study:

Fifty percent of a group of attentive students will remember half of what was said the first five minutes of a lecture.

In the second five minutes of the lecture, retention drops to only 25 percent.

Fifteen minutes after the lecture, less than one-half of one percent will remember the facts of a verbal presentation correctly.

The churches of our world have pastors preaching for one to two hours. The president of the U.S. talks on TV for an hour at a time. Executives of major conglomerates will lecture to their middle management hour upon hour.

Who believes these survey, studies, and research projects? Do we, or don't we?

A recent survey reported that in examining the personal history of the top one hundred corporations in our country, one particular factor appeared in each of the studies. Its occurrence was almost double the next reported fact: fathers of CEO's had a common profile item—they were alcoholics.

A quirky mind at an MBA school might request students to encourage their fathers to drink. It portends a great future.

General Tire's CEO

Mr. O. was the President and CEO of the General Tire Company. He would appoint as his first vice president an active Mason, who was also known for his strong Protestant Church activities. His assistant would be a Catholic, a member of the Knights of Columbus. Mr. O. alternated. All down the line: Mason- KC; Mason-KC. This practice discouraged loyalty to the immediate superior. When an employee did get a promotion, it was always two grades. The fellow, who was promoted, jumped over the man in front of him. He did this to Masons and Knights of Columbus alike. The employee's loyalty was to be to the company and not to the immediate boss.

Quite some years ago, General Tire held a sales meeting at the old Edgewater Beach Hotel on the Lake Michigan shoreline in Chicago. It was after World War II and over 1500 tire salesmen were brought into their convention. Mr. O., with his gargantuan-sized ego, conducted it almost alone. At times a few men from the home office were permitted short moments to speak. Invariably, their talks were interrupted and corrected by O'Neil, at times in the middle of a sentence. Mr. O. was all wise, all knowing. He was a very difficult man to be near, much less work for.

At a question and answer session, a salesman asked why General Tire did not have any Jewish dealers. Mr. O. answered, "Everyone knows the Jews are smarter and sharper than the Irish, so why do business with someone when I knew I was going to lose."

A dealer from Mississippi wanted to know why the Squeegee Tire was so high priced. It was difficult to sell General Squeegee Tires in Mississippi. Mr. O's answer was "We don't manufacture Squeegees to sell to niggers." He had a complete lack of feeling or empathy for any and all. That was President O.

The Korean War was raging at that time and that created some voids and shortages in a wide range of base supplies. Dupont made fabric for the entire tire industry. That fabric was designed to withstand the constant flexing that occurs every time a car tire rolls. It was made for a soft ride. Another factory made fabric for truck tires. The fabrics do look alike, but each is made for a particular use. A truck tire is solid; it uses one hundred pounds of air pressure while a passenger tire is soft at thirty pounds or less. That information is common knowledge to any and all that have had contact in the tire industry.

The passenger tire fabric was on short supply and all tire companies put their dealers on a quota system. Tires were scarce, and prices soared. However, Mr. O. could get all the truck tire fabric he could use. He decided to make Squeegees tires from truck tire fabric and they failed. Oh, how they failed!

Almost 90 percent of Squeegee Tire production failed. The tire dealer would replace each tire at no cost to the customer, and then the dealer would get $5.00 for each tire adjustment made. It helped pay the salaries of the service men at all the dealerships.

At the same Edgewater Beach Convention, Mr. O. went to the mike and was extolling and praising the safety and quality inherent in all Squeegees. The salesmen erupted into loud guffaws and belly laughs. Amazingly, the President of General enthusiastically sang the praises of Squeegee safety. What a sense of humor!

Mr. O. stopped and turned to his vice president, Mr. P., and asked, "What the hell are these horses' Asses laughing about?" Mr. P., red faced, said, "Call a coffee break and I'll tell you."

It was over coffee that Mr. O. first learned of his colossal failure. It was his definite decision to use truck fabric when all knew better. No one had told him the results. No one had the guts to step forward and tell Mr. O. that his decision created unbelievable problems.

Montgomery Wards

Our country has been blessed with CEOs, who by whatever means, see to it that their organization grows steadily successful over the years. But, there are many whose foresight for whatever reason was muddled, fuzzy, poorly conceived.

Mr. A. of Montgomery Wards is a sad example of that type of CEO. Back in the 1940s there were two giant mail order catalog houses. One was Wards; the second was Sears. They were relatively close in dollar volume. Wards was worth 300 million and Sears 400 million.

Mr. A. reigned at Wards, and he believed to the depths of his being that a depression was coming and not a war. The isolationism of the Midwest helped produce this attitude. The goal he had in mind was to hold back expansion, conserve all assets, increase Wards' cash position. When the bad times would hit, Wards would buy out Sears who by then would have succumbed to bankruptcy. It never happened.

In 1967 Wards disappeared from the Big Board on the Stock Exchange. Mobil Oil was now Wards' parent organization. From 1940 to 1967 Wards' volume doubled to 600 million. During that identical period Sears grew from 400 million to 9 billion. Sears had increased its original worth eighteen fold.

Far too often we find these failure-prone CEO's will be given a "golden umbrella" at retirement. These words imply gigantic severance pay rewards to individuals who do not deserve such treatment; to be rewarded for failure seems ridiculous.

Wards is a classic example of an organization bragging to one and all that it is super conservative. This basically cautious attitude of the CEO was ever hesitant to be creative or innovative. This do little or do nothing attitude brought on its constant decline. Today Wards is no more!

It Costs More

The General Tire and Rubber company of Akron, Ohio can state truthfully that it got its start in a horse and wagon operation that old Grandpa O'Neill worked when he first came to Ohio from Ireland. His operation was basic. Whatever the farmers and their wives wanted to buy, he sold them. If it wasn't on the wagon this trip, it was there the next.

As Ford and other auto companies grew in Detroit, so did Firestone, Goodyear, and Goodrich Tire companies in Akron. As more and more Ohio farm boys moved to Akron to work in the rubber factories, Grandpa O'Neill's business escalated, amazingly so! Pots and pans, socks and shoes, sheets and diapers. You name it. O'Neill had it. Only now, the wagon was long gone and a huge department store developed and expanded. The one store grew to many stores in nearby cities.

Most Irish families have trouble keeping their sons in line. The competitive spirit is so strong; each wants to be first. Grandpa O'Neill had the same problem. But he had an answer! He bought out the old McCreary Tire and Rubber Company in Kansas City and sent his son, William, to run it. Tom, his other son, stayed at the store. William lost a million in 1929 and another in 1930. Grandpa said, "You'd better move the plant to Akron. Rubber companies don't lose money here."

General Tire didn't rock the boat of the other tire companies when it first moved to Akron. Young William said, "Merchandising I learned from my father, and I think I can make some of it work in the tire business." As a young man, home in the summertime from Holy Cross University, he had worked in the men's department of his father's store, O'Neil's. He soon discovered that his dad would purchase some ties for 50 cents and price them at $1.00.

He bought better ties for 75 cents and sold them for $2.50. The best ties cost him $1.00 and those he sold for $10.00. A basic belief the O'Neills had all of their lives was one that most Americans believe: if it costs more money, it must be worth more.

Repeat.

Most Americans believe that because something costs more it must be worth more.

There really is no mystery in the manufacturing of tires. Dupont makes all the fabric for all tire companies. U.S. Steel makes all the steel wire that is used in the tire beads. The rubber content is identical in each tire corporation. McNeil Tire Molding Co. makes all the molds for all the companies, but each will have its own design imbedded in the walls of the mold. All workers belong to the same union. Same. Same. Same.

Bill O'Neill remembering his "ties" experience at his father's store made the General Squeegee Dune 90. It has had different names during different time periods. The tire weighed about 10 percent more than original equipment tires. Bill O'Neill priced it 100 percent more than other tire brands on the market.

If it costs more, it must be worth more.

And America bought it.

MBAs

M.B.A.

All of us recognize the initials MBA as meaning Master of Business Administration. But some employees, frustrated by bungling misdirection, interpret them to mean *More Baloney for America*. The following chapter will list a few remarkable performances in scattered industries. Some so catastrophic that you wonder, *"Did it just happen, or was the misdirection intentional?"*

When a major company brings aboard a new MBA, he is encouraged to spend time in all its facilities and plants. Usually the new hires are friendly personalities and encourage the employees to discuss their woes and successes both on and off the job. These coffee break sessions are like diving for *"pearls."* But the pearls are bits and pieces of what is good and what is bad. He finds workers with twenty, thirty, even forty years of work experience, telling him what will work and what won't work.

His job now is to cull out the plausible, the sensible, the workable ideas. A good CEO should listen to his workers. Japan has taught us that. But our hard-nosed, independent CEOs still do not manage like the Japanese. United States bosses hire MBAs at substantial salaries to help improve company profits. If perchance a prospective student reads the brochures that our United States business schools produce, he might be stunned and amazed at some of the subtitles for a given course. Harvard, some time ago, listed one that would catch your eye: *How to cut the rungs out of the ladder of the man ahead of you without his knowing it.* Quite a statement!

Harvard, a school founded by Rev. John Harvard, did have a Christian foundation. One cannot but wonder what happened to its Christian beginning. Most all of our business schools teach each student the complete package: how to dress; how to write a resume that will get a job; how to survive in an unpleasant environment. Ninety percent of the curriculum goals will fall under the initials C.Y.A. (cover your ass). Ten percent will teach the values an MBA can deliver. We seem not to really know how all this came to be.

Over 300 years ago, a Jesuit named Father Gracia 1601-1658, developed a philosophy that even to this day is most appropriate. It wasn't just developed after World War II. Read it slowly. It applies today. As I remember it, it goes something like this.

1. What brings credit? Look to it yourself. What brings discredit? Look to another to do it in your stead.

2. Embark on another man's business to save yourself from thinking of your own.

3. Trust your friends today as if they will be your enemies of tomorrow.

4. Know how to sweeten your refusals and learn how to find the right thumb screw so that no man can refuse you.

5. Keep your eyes fixed on a happy outcome since a victor need never excuse himself

6. Do things in a human way as if there were no Godly way and do things in a Godly way as if there were no human way.

Guess human greed and selfishness has been around a long time.

An MBA and Dog Food

Some sales meetings can be a complete surprise to management, plant managers, office personnel and the sales team. Chicago had a company named Rival Dog Food. It were bought out by one of our nation's giant conglomerates. Naturally an MBA was brought in to up-grade the company.

The recent Harvard MBA graduate announced at a general meeting his sales plan for the coming year. In the past Rival had 11 percent of the Chicago market. That figure would be doubled to 22 percent. A 100 percent growth in one year. The five-year plan was so grandiose that the Chicago dog population would have to multiply by 500 percent to make his projections plausible.

First, to the sales department. The sales force was upgraded from driving Chevrolets to Buicks. Then he doubled the bonuses from 5 percent to 10 percent. The next step was the complete revamping of the manufacturing plant with brand new assembly and packaging equipment. This was necessary to keep up with the planned growth in volume. Packaging designers were hired, and they won a packaging award for their efforts. The advertising budget was doubled; more TV and radio spots and larger newspaper ads were added. He hired a new advertising agency to do all this. He ordered a new facade for the building and an office equipment designer spent a fortune in glamorizing the home office decor.

One year went by. At the yearly sales meeting the CEO stood up to address the entire group. Obviously he was a disturbed and flustered man and he started to shout. "Didn't I put you salesmen in Buicks? Didn't I double your bonuses? Didn't we hire a new advertising agency and double the advertising budget? Didn't we completely revamp and overhaul the manufacturing facilities? Didn't we completely redo the offices and put a new front on the building? Didn't we win a packaging award? We still have 11 percent of the market, as much as we had when all this started. All this! "By now his face had turned from red to purple. "What the Hell is wrong?" he screamed. A voice from the back of the room said softly, "The dogs won't eat the damn stuff."

An MBA Fortune

There are two very distinctive schools of thought regarding the selling profession. Some organizations with MBAs or accountants, who become CEOs, have one basic formula. *It,* meaning sales, is done by the numbers. Specific selling phrases are mouthed by a given number of salesmen. They in turn make a specific number of calls on specific accounts at specific times. All by the numbers.

It does work in *specific* cases. It does work for beans and bread, toothpaste and school paste, nails and pails. All the humdrum items kept in bins and drawers are the products for these CEOs. Our world could not go on without all these items that help us live our lives.

But there are innumerable new developments, new products, new ideas and discoveries. They must be introduced by a sales *artist.* These salesmen neither live nor work by the numbers. They dream, improvise, and discover new and unusual uses for a product or service. Each salesman must learn for himself which category is correct for him. At times a company will start from scratch with a hard driving creative sales *artist.* Rarely does a new concern ever succeed if the management sets a policy of doing it by the numbers. Some of these companies will grow, make money and lo and behold in comes an MBA or an accountant to become president.

The SVE Education Materials company over a 12 to 15 year program hired **a** group of sales *artists.* The president was also an *artist.* It was a well-run company and a $6 million total volume produced a $3 million net profit. Almost unbelievable.

The MBAs took over. The *artists* were replaced by cookie salesmen. The total sales force went from fifty to almost one hundred. The volume did grow to $17 million. The profit went from $3 million to $1 million.

The Singer Corporation created this problem.

What to do? The SVE division was sold. Survive? It didn't! Neither did Singer.

Sales Meetings

SALES MEETINGS

As dedicated professionals, most salesmen will constantly approach each sales meeting with the open-mind attitude that they, personally, will be rewarded by a gem. The gem might be just one or two fine points on the diamond scale, but it will add to their skills, technique, and knowledge.

Meeting after meeting, the same litany is constantly repeated: Know your product; know your customer; know your territory, and always be prepared!

Whatever job a salesman holds, it is the same daily routine. The sameness creates a lackadaisical attitude. Sales meeting can be a refresher course. Spring training in baseball, medical seminars for doctors, the list goes on.

The truth is that new techniques, new products, new advertising schemes are introduced. But it is also true that the proven skills and techniques are always reviewed thoroughly and never ignored or forgotten.

Each organization will assemble their sales force to comply with its own needs. Some have national assemblies, others regional, and some by-product lines if that company is so diversified. In all such meetings, a common factor exists:

all salesmen are different. Tall, short, thin, fat, old, young, ever on. But each man has something to add to the repertoire if salesmen are wise enough and smart enough to ask the right questions.

Salesmen, like the rest of us, are always flattered by someone asking for advice or information. When we think it through, we are complimenting a man indirectly by letting him know he has answered our need. All of us have stories of success and horror and each is a lesson of experience—a gem that will be ours forever.

These short episodes tell of a wide range of sales meetings, goals set by the company, and show the strange style of each meeting. Read on!

A Sales Manager to Remember

When I went to work for the General Tire and Rubber Company in 1948, that was my first encounter with Alcoholics Anonymous (AA).

The sales training manager, Mr. S. was a dedicated member of AA. He was a rugged, warm, and friendly man. His piercing, all-knowing eyes seemed to look directly into our inner selves. Just like Willie Nelson! Eyes that seemed to say, "I've been there. I've done that. There are no surprises!"

At a sales meeting we soon learned that Mr. S. was born in rural Ohio-near Akron. He had spent his entire working life in the tire business.

At that first session, he told a story I've remembered all of my life. As a boy he and his friends would draw a huge circle on the side of a bam. Then they would take a shovel and scoop up some cow plop and hurl it at the target. Hitting the circle was not as important as how much plop you could make stick. Similarly, a good salesperson soon recognizes the best measure of a sales presentation is how much the presenter can make stick. Mr. S. had a way with words.

Over the years, we kept in touch. Bits and pieces of information helped me fill in the puzzle that showed what Mr. S. was all about. Eventually, I came to know, admire and respect this fine, fine man. The unbelievable impact that automobile production had on Detroit also created the impetus for Akron's growth from a small country town to a thriving tire producing major city. Rural Ohio farm boys streamed into

Akron, hungry for employment. Mr. S. was one of those boys. His first job was on the assembly line manning a tire mould. It was a fiercely hot, dirty, smelly and noisy job. With steam lines hissing and pneumatic airlines popping and screaming, it was almost a living hell. The tire moulds would open their jaw-like mouths and into it a worker would insert the black doughnut shape tire. These tires were pre-assembled from fabric, steel beads, and rubber. The mold would be closed and the tire would be cooked, baked, cured. You name it.

When approaching a tire plant, the strong acrid stench of rubber being cured is long remembered. But humankind has the tremendous ability to adapt. After a short stay, the stink goes unnoticed.

Mr. S. paid his dues and being the warm, friendly person he is, he was promoted to sales and finally on to sales training manager. He married his childhood sweetheart and soon they had a son and a daughter. This fine family moved to suburban Akron into a two story Georgian; he had two cars and a horse-shoe driveway. Theirs was the good life. Pearl Harbor disrupted Mr. S's life just as it did the lives of all of us. His young son, Tom, was a junior at Akron University. He was an active participant in the Naval ROTC program. In the spring of '42 Tom was ordered down to Pensacola, Florida to a naval pilot training program. Naturally, Tom was thrilled and his family proud. Our government was speeding up the pilot training program. Fliers were needed now! Tom was an early victim of this hastiness. Less than sixty days after arriving at Pensacola, Tom's plane crashed and he was killed.

Mrs. S. and her daughter Susan obtained special gas rationing coupons and immediately drove down to Pensacola to pick up the body. In 1942 our country did not have the super highways that exist today. The roads were two lanes. Their car crashed head on into an on coming truck. Mother and daughter were both killed instantly. In just twenty-four hours, Mr. S. lost his entire family: wife, son, and daughter. He escaped into a bottle and on into oblivion, spending the next five years on Akron's Market Street.

All big cities have their areas taken over by the homeless and the drunks. New York has its Bowery; Chicago its Madison St.; Los Angeles its Broadway, and Akron has Market St.

Back in 1932 the banks took over Goodyear Rubber Company and gave a golden umbrella to a man we'll call Mr. B. who was the majority stockholder. They gave him the funds to start a small tire company. Mr. B., a widower, had only one son, Bob, who was both the apple of his eye and a worrisome heartbreak. Bob was a drunk. He drank to get drunk and succeeded day in and day out. Over the years Bob's dad tried every known tactic and technique: sanitariums, anti-abuse, you name it. Reading about Alcoholic's Anonymous success rate, Mr. B decided to try that. Down to Market St. he went and picked up six of the worst, and they were the worst, smelly, stumbling, incoherent, gaunt men. The word "men" is a misnomer. They were absolutely nothing.

He drove these six drunks back to his castle-like mansion far from town. The six stayed the night. The next morning Bob came down to the spacious dining room that could seat twenty.

Bob's father insisted that breakfast together was a must. The old man sat one end and Bob at the other. There were three drunks on one side and three on the other. Bob, bloody eyed and bloated, shouted at his dad. "What the hell is wrong with you? Where in God's name did you find these bums?"

His dad's answer went right for the kill. "If it wasn't for my money, this is what you would look like." That was the beginning of the first "AA" local in Akron.

Bob lived a day at a time with the sure, solemn prayer ''I will not take a drink today." It wasn't easy; it did take time. The six drunks and Bob talked and talked. Gallons of coffee seemed to be part of the AA ritual. All made their way to sobriety except one, who got up in the middle of the night and disappeared.

Mr. S. was one of the men who made it. In the ten years we were in contact never did I meet an individual who gave such concern, funds, time and energy to help both men and women sober up. Addiction has an almost insurmountable hold on those it captures. It is one thing to say, "I'll stop," and another to do so. Far too many fail that first step of AA.

A question that has gone unanswered all these years: Was Mr. S. always a fine, fine man? Or did that violent catastrophe in '42 when he lost his entire family create the man, temper his soul, and produce the Mr. S. I admired? At any rate, he was one of the finest of men.

Memory

In a lifetime of selling that encompasses literally hundreds of sales meetings, the variety of themes are as unique and as different as the fingerprints of those who conduct these sessions. One year Dayton Tire chose *memory* as its main topic. It was inspirational. It opened the eyes of all the participants to appreciate how some develop and use their brains.

Dayton Tire presented a film showing George Marshall conducting a press meeting during WWII. At least fifty reporters were bombarding him with questions about weapons, manpower, and shortages. Some reporters asked two or three questions. Marshall had an astute mind, along with the most disciplined of work habits. He was a truly honest, dedicated human being. But he had no charisma! Sober faced, straight forward he managed and controlled these press sessions. There are too few people who can demand respect and control press release sessions as Marshall could.

He would listen to all the questions hurled at him and would answer none until all the queries ended. Then he would begin his answers directing his eyes and his words at the reporter who had asked the question. It was an inspiration to watch this wondrous solid, sober-faced general conduct the sessions. His memory was working to the utmost degree.

Then we watched another short film about Jerry Lucas, the Ohio State and professional basketball player with a phenomenal memory. At one time he memorized the Manhattan Telephone Book. Ridiculous? Perhaps, but he did it. Jerry was almost driven to sharpen his memory. He would count the telephone poles outside the train's window as it sped between Cleveland and New York.

Obviously, those of us participating in these sessions recognized that the two men were in a class by themselves. But the rest of can improve the memory skills we have. A good memory can be honed. A fine talent for all salesmen to cultivate. The public library has title upon title on its shelves.

As a good, successful professional, salesmen should work to remember the names of customers on whom they make repeat calls. A sales pitch should be both coherent and to the point. A customer does recognize and appreciate effective sales presentations.

National Cash Register

Many sales organizations do a detailed training of their new salesmen. The insurance and pharmaceutical companies in particular are outstanding. But none surpass the National Cash Register Company. Cash Registers are as varied as the stores to which they are sold: restaurants have different requirements than taverns; department stores are not the same as a local candy shops, the variety of needs is endless. NCR in Dayton, Ohio conducted endless surveys studying how their products were sold. Their sale training manuals were detailed to a precise wording of the sales pitch. The company knows what it wants its salesmen to say and do. All this is the background for NCR's particular sales training program.

A constant, consistent sales training is conducted on a weekly basis. All salesmen play the role of either the customer or the NCR salesman. They actually had a raised platform stage with desks and counter props. To set the scene, the trainer identifies the type of customer. Each and every retail operation has its own unique problems and needs. When an NCR salesman has studied and grasped the material in all the manuals, he can quickly respond with the proper answers to any and all of the customer's questions.

Proper to NCR is just one way—*the NCR way*. When a customer said "hello," there was a specific response. "Good Morning" received another. No variation of responses was ever permitted.

At times the sales manager would play the role of the customer. When he willed it, the session could become very awkward and disturbing for the NCR salesman. The salesman would stutter and stammer. Fumbling for the *proper* response, he might be embarrassed. The rest of the sales force was the audience sitting in the theatre type seats and muttering or chuckling at the performance. To make a damned fool of yourself in front of your peers is the ultimate of embarrassment.

One Saturday the Sales Manager was in a particularly ugly mood. He put a new man named George on stage. The scene was set. George was a fine looking, husky type University of Illinois graduate, very personable, athletic, warm—a well-rounded man. But he had a severe temper. As George started to fumble for the proper answer, the manager became more caustic. The questions became vicious The sarcasm grew. The tone of voice more strident. George's face turned red, then purple. By this time his fellow salesmen were roaring. The muttering and slight chuckles grew to belly laughs. George was furious and exploded! He reached over and grabbed the sales manager by the lapels and punched him right in the face, knocking him off the stage into the laps of the salesmen. Naturally, George was fired.

If there is any justice to this tale, NCR fired the manager two weeks later. He had carried his sales training too far.

Obfuscation

In the 70's, the word linguistics became a buzz word to teachers, superintendents and educational sales people. One night, for no particular reason, the Midwest manager sent an interoffice memo to his president. With tongue in cheek, he asked the question, "Why does the educational industry say linguistic? Why not *linguastics*?" His argument was based on the word gymnastics. If that is proper form, linguistics should be *linguastics*.

The President, a pompous individual, did not pick up on the humor in the report.

His mind-set allowed no fun to creep in and grow. He immediately fired off long inquiries to editors-in-chief of all the major text book publishers: Scott Foresman American Book, Silver Burdett, Harcourt Brace, Encyclopedia Britannica. They were some of the giants. He missed few. Within two to three weeks answers were salvoed back. Some rambled on to ten and twelve pages. If it wasn't much to do about nothing, it was much ado about little. Every editor welcomed the opportunity to show his scholarship and supposed dedication to quality in the education market. These men possessed mountainous egos that blossomed in the rarefied air atop the pristine pinnacles of the publishing industry.

Our president made photocopies of each and every document. They were not treated as reports; they were documents. Every single one was forwarded to the Midwest manager for his edification. They were received in glee. The manager shared the documents from the pompous pundits with all the sales reps in his division. All this bantering about their industry's shallow and superficial worship of seldom used words and phrases triggered an idea in the quirky mind of the Midwest manager. The five regional managers were expected to give a short talk at each National Sales Meeting. He would give one that would sound good and say nothing. To make it more effective, his regional salesmen were instructed to cheer when he pointed a finger and to laugh when he held up both hands. This is the speech he gave:

The educational industry must be responsive to incremental capability. We need a total monitored time-phase or balanced logistical hardware. Some believe it might be best to have systematized, third generation options. To settle for integrated, management programming might be better than parallel, digital projection. It is not simple for functional, organizational flexibility to combat optional, transitional concepts. Possibly our industry needs synchronized, reciprocal mobility or a compatible policy contingency.

The Midwest salesmen cheered and laughed on cue; the rest of the group of one hundred men listened and clapped when the speech ended. You can't help but wonder who does listen.

The following is a list of words the Midwestern salesman used for his speech. By combing and recombining one word from each column, it is possible to create and endless number of pompous, stilted, erudite sentences that are "non understandable." Try it!

a. equalization

b. creating

c. capacity

d. monitorize

e. consolidation

f. compatible

g. synchronize

h. transient

i. Contingent

j. mathematics

k. transitional

l. second generation

m. functionalize

n. optional

o. mobilization

p. reciprocities

q. projectiles

r. concepts

s. flexibility

t. revitalization

u. inconceivable

Poor Decisions

POOR DECISIONS

Management American style is a constant quest for bigger and bigger profit margins. Production lines are fully automated using less and less manpower. Advertising departments have been given almost unlimited funds for television, radio, and print media. The profits level off.

Apple Juice

The story of the antics of a food company is one example of the lengths management will go to in its search for more profit. A line of baby food had a countless variety of products. Visit your local supermarket and you will be astounded by the variety of tiny jars.

When manufacturing techniques reach their peak efficiency and advertising can do no more, where does management turn to increase profits? To the product itself. First, apple juice was watered down. No one reacted. Babies couldn't tell you it was tasteless. The watering down continued. The day finally arrived when apple juice was nothing more than colored water. An unknown someone blew the whistle. There was a trial. The food company was found guilty. The fine was nominal.

A just decision could have been made. The CEO of the baby food company should have been force-fed his own apple juice until he died!

Selling Subterfuge

When a salesman gets involved in *sharp practice*, no actual stealing occurs, but the customer does not purchase what he thinks he bought. This sales episode took place in a major music store in downtown Chicago. The customer had made more than a few calls at the store and finally came to a firm conclusion. The piano would be a Kimball Baby Grand. In some ways major music purchases are subject to the same bargaining that goes on in automobile salesrooms. Trade in? Firm price? Delivery charges?

The customer mailed in a substantial down payment on the piano to be ordered from the factory. She requested that she would come to the store and check the baby grand before it was delivered to her home. Six weeks went by and the customer was finally called. It happened that the cartage company had put a huge scratch across the top of the brand new piano. The customer played it and announced that the tone was perfect, but refused to accept it. The scratch was ugly.

It was agreed that a new top would be ordered from the factory. It would take four weeks for the replacement to be shipped to the store. After it was received she returned to the store. The piano looked brand new. But when she played it, her face screwed up into an ugly grimace. She said the sound was horrible and refused to accept the piano. She wanted another.

The salesman, a quick thinker, said, "Let me look at our future deliveries." He came back and told the woman that a suburban store would have the exact same model the following week. The piano was moved from the downtown store out to their suburban location. Our finicky customer went there, played the piano and found it perfect. She said, "I'm sure all of you can hear the difference."

The piano was the exact same one she had played before, but it had been moved to a new location. It's a fact of life; some customers have trouble making a purchase. Some sales take a lot of patience

The automobile industry has developed car salesmen who seem to enjoy cheating the customer, even when the customer pays full list price for a car that is loaded with ridiculous extras. The salesman will switch tires or the radio and add on special delivery charges.

The list of ploys is endless. The genes and bloodlines of these salesmen seem to be identical to the genes of the men who rustled cattle or stole horses in our not too distant past. The new car business is ruthless, but the used car business is disgusting. That word is far too mild. It is rotten.

Most Americans recognize all the tricks of changing tires, floor mats, spinning the speedometer back, hiding bent frames, putting extra thick oil in the crankcase to muffle the noisy engine pistons. The mechanical tricks to hides the defects of used cars are endless. The paperwork becomes a jungle of disinformation and misfortune. More than we like to admit, a used car that was taken in trade for $ 1,000 is priced on the lot at $2,000.

The customer at times gives a down payment of a $1,000 on a used car worth $1,000. In his mind he wants to pay $100 per month for 12 months, which is $1,200. His down payment of $1,000 has him paying $2,200 for a car that was traded in at $ 1,000.

That's not all.

When the papers finally come to the house, he finds he owes $ 100 per month for 24 months. Now he is paying $3,600 for that $1,000 car. To rub salt in the wounds, used car salesmen are in their glory.

At times a car lot will have two identical cars, same year, model, make and color. One is a good used car. Their term—*cream puff.* The other is a dog! The customer, after going through all the steps of buying a car, down payment, credit check, signed forms is told to return the next evening. His car will get its final check.

He returns the next evening. Delivery is often made in the dark. All the final papers have been signed and he drives home.

The next morning in the bright sunshine he wonders what happened. Is he losing his eyesight? The sharp customer will then check the car numbers against the numbers on the contract. They do check out. Another used car salesman had a good day. It is easier than rustling cattle in the old days.

Two Men—Same Job

Two salesmen were sitting in a school superintendent's office in the Washington, D.C. area. Probably the most annoying part of any sales job, other than making out reports, is waiting to see the customer.

After introducing themselves, they made the usual small talk. They chatted about marital status, number of kids, and place of residence. Each man admitted he was new to the job and also new to the area. Both expressed hope that they might come up with insights about particular sales patterns and knowledge about which school districts had the most funds. Both knew that educational materials were their common ground. Finally, one man asked the other, "*What kind of educational materials do you sell?* Both sold filmstrips. To top that, they both worked for the same company, the Jim Handy Co.

A man named Jamieson Handy started the company with the usual set-up—sales manager, advertising manager, etc., but every now and then Jamieson Handy would do things without telling anyone. It was *his* company—lock, stock and barrel. He could do what he wanted and he did.

Jamieson Handy hired a salesman, a man he met in an accidental encounter. He sat next to a likable man on an airplane. Handy hired him on the spot, sent him samples, gave him advertising literature, etc. He did all this without telling anyone at the office. But his sales manager had already hired a new man for the same position. Now what to do? Handy fired both of them!

Salesmen do not have much job security in their lives. What an understatement!

A CEO's Error

Most major corporations insist that they have testing procedures for all their products because they want to be positive that the product will deliver complete satisfaction to the customer. Actually too many companies send their product out to the market as it is produced. The market is where it is tested.

If too many failures developed in the first ninety days, the company will either stop production, change formulas, or develop procedures or techniques to correct those errors. The United States consumer is the guinea pig and just as long as the company makes good on its guarantee, we continue to buy the product.

During the Korean War when Mr. O. was at the helm of the a tire and rubber company; he made a monumental mistake. Over the years, the company with a huge advertising budget, created in the minds of the United States market a top-flight image for its Squeegee tire. It was a top profit maker for the company. The cost of raw materials was about 100 percent over the average tire, the equipment tire. Pricing was the factor that produced the profit. A customer paid double the amount of any original equipment tire.

The strong advertising budget hammered home the image that it was top quality and because it costs more, it must be worth more. But double the price? It wasn't worth it! The Korean War created shortages of all products. The fabric needed to make passenger tires was in short supply. Truck tire fabric was not short. It was available.

Mr. O. said, "Let's use truck tire fabric to make our Squeegee Tire." He was President and CEO and as always, everyone followed his commands without question. Almost immediately the Squeegee Tire, the top of the line, started to blow out. The branch in Oak Park, Illinois had one memorable customer. He was an Italian undertaker on Chicago's West Side. He had over thirty tire failures on one hearse.

The tire failures were called zippers. When the tire was dismounted you could look inside and find the fabric separated in a straight 12" to 18" line running parallel to the tread. Truck tires are inflated to 100 pounds of air pressure, and the tire does not flex. It is solid. Passenger tires use 30 pounds of air pressure and flex to give the passengers a soft ride.

Mr. O. ran a rigid and tough company. Criticism was not allowed. No "faults" were ever admitted, much less discussed. After almost one year of 90 percent failure of the nation's most costly tire, this problem finally came to Mr. O's attention.

He was making a keynote speech at a national sales meeting. It was held at the old Edgewater Beach Hotel in Chicago. He was remarking on the quality and profitability of the Squeegee Tire. Fifteen hundred salesmen started to laugh. He stopped and asked, "What the hell are you laughing at?" The audience roared. Mr. O. was quite a card poking fun at his own problems. Not so! He just didn't know! He did find out that day and production was stopped. Not knowing was his own fault. All who worked for Mr. O. were afraid to point out his colossal error. There was a definite reason for the two types of tire fabric, but he had ignored it.

General Motors

When we observe the growth of our corporate conglomerates, both nationally and then internationally, we can't help but wonder. Does loyalty and patriotism to a country exist in a corporation? Or do corporations in their quest for profits jump over geographic and national boundaries? General Motors is probably a good example of America's worldwide corporate image. It employs many, many people producing a fair to passable product and in most years shows growth and pays dividends.

Prior to World War II, General Motors expanded into Europe and opened a huge facility in Germany. This business of loyalty and patriotism now enters the picture. Our U.S. tanks could neither stand up to the firepower nor to the strength of the Nazi tanks. The Nazi tanks were superior. They were better than the United States tanks built by General Motors' plants in Detroit, Michigan. Ask any GI who served in World War II and he will spell that out. That's only part of the story.

The United States 8th Air Force, along with the British, bombed the hell out of Germany and eventually the General Motors plant was leveled, bombed out. There was nothing left. Eventually, the Nazis were defeated. Some years after World War II, General Motors decided to sue the United States government for 250 million dollars for damages to their European German facility. GM won that lawsuit.

We wonder would GM sue the Nazi government if Detroit had been bombed?

An "Impossible Request"

Robert Burns said in one of his poems, "The best laid schemes o'mice and men gang aft agley." (Often go wrong). During the Vietnam War a shortage of capable, efficient factory workers developed. Our armed forces had recruited thousands of young males who usually held the entry-level jobs in our factories.

Our congress made special funds available for vocational training. To get these grants it was necessary to submit a detailed report. These projects listed specific objectives, the available facilities and the personnel involved. The school system of Columbus, Ohio had all the needed criteria. A large group of young males, 18 to 23, who had dropped out of school, were unemployed and unemployable. (They were functionally illiterate, reading below 3d grade level) and had a lack of discipline, which was evident in tardiness, poor listening skills, and inability to follow directions.)

Columbus has Ohio State University with its famous Engineering Department, and also the Battle Institute. The renowned *think tank has* over four hundred Ph.D.s on its staff. Their most recognized invention was the Xerox process. Royalties on this patent alone have gone a long way to finance Battle's projects. The Columbus Board of Education had a large building in the downtown area that was available and could easily handle one thousand students. A $750 thousand project was warranted. Eight Ph.D.s volunteered to help write the program.

Washington D.C.'s Education Department was impressed with the credentials of these men, as well as the facilities and the ultimate goal, and quickly gave the okay to take one thousand men off the streets and help them fill needed positions in Columbus. A luncheon meeting was called and the Ph.D.s were advised that the one thousand students, because of poor academic records, were "drop-outs."

The idea was proposed that maybe audio/visual materials could be found to teach chemistry, physics and electricity. Audio/visual could be film, video, filmstrips, cassettes, and pictures. An educational representative who had broad experience in this field was asked to help these Ph.D.'s pick and choose helpful materials.

First point specified: *Third grade vocabulary should be used in all the study material.* The rep's reply was, "Please take another look at what you have said. You want to teach specific problems in chemistry, physics and electricity using third grade vocabulary? Don't you think you should teach reading first?"

The consensus of all in attendance was that the project did not have the time to increase the reading level of the one thousand men to be trained. The project stuttered and sputtered and eventually failed. Another $750 thousand of federal funds went for naught.

Gasoline and Electricity

Back in the early days of automobile, S. F. Bowser of Fort Wayne, Indiana obtained United States patents that proved his pumps could draw gasoline from underground tanks and pump the gasoline into the automobiles in precise, measured gallons. In a few years the company grew until it shipped and billed $270 million worth of tanks and pumps in 1926.

The following letter was written in 1927:

Jan. 4, 1927
Fort Wayne, Indiana
TO: ALL SALES PERSONNEL:
FROM: S. F. BOWSER

It has come to my attention that we have competition that will use electrical motors to pump gasoline.

It is the considered opinion of your company's Board of Directors and myself that gasoline and electricity cannot mix. There will be gas stations exploding all over the United States. It is folly to think that such foolish ideas can succeed

Sincerely,
S.F BOWSER

The S. F. Bowser Company went from $270 million in 1926 to $250 million in 1927. The Wayne Electric Pump was safe, and they took all the business away from Bowser!

Another example that CEOs can make stupid mistakes like the rest of us.

Two Singers in South Bend

When the Singer Sewing Machine Company fired eighty hundred employees and leveled the factory and made it into a parking lot, it wouldn't take a genius to see the impact such a layoff would have on the town's economy. All of it. Shortly after that the Studebaker Corporation moved most of its operations to Canada and closed all facilities at South Bend. This closing was a death knell to the town's economy.

The General Tire Franchise dealer, Don Singer, was a hard working, intelligent, ambitious man. His operation was flawless, but with a majority of South Bend's labor force unemployed, his sales plummeted. Massive firings like Singer Sewing Machine plus Studebaker's closing created havoc.

When quotas set by home offices were not met, the usual, the normal, the consistent action by all corporations was to fire the individual involved. The circumstances behind the deep drop in volume were never permitted to change that decision. Missed quota—out you go! Sam Poor was the treasurer of General Tire. All the O'Neill sons called him Uncle Sam, but there was no blood between them. As treasurer, Mr. Poor had the difficult task of closing down a franchise when it got into financial difficulties. A franchise tire dealer considers himself the owner of his local business. And he is. Except when the manufacturer stops shipping you the product, what do you own?

The following is a rough copy of Sam Poor's letter:

Dear Don Singer:

First, I want to thank you for your warm hospitality on my recent trip to South Bend. That home cooked meal your wife made was truly a joy. I especially loved her homemade apple pie with ice cream. Your two sons must make you and your wife proud to see how well they turned out.

May you and your family have a fine Christmas and may the New Year bring you all the best.

It is necessary at this time to advise you that as of January 1st, you will no longer have a General Tire Franchise.

Sincerely,
Sam Poor

Don Singer took on a B.F. Goodrich and being the conservative hardworking man, he survived. He framed that letter and read it every day for the next ten years. General Tire eventually returned to Don Singer and wanted him back on their team. That framed letter and ten years of daily reading gave him the strength and guts to drive a hard bargain. Don Singer finally had his revenge!

Don Singer, now a General Tire Dealer, insisted that the framed copy of Sam Poor's letter would continue to hang prominently on the wall in his office. A daily reminder that it is always possible to get such a letter.

An Order Shredder

In the late sixties any company in the educational business enjoyed phenomenal growth. Both volume and profits leaped skyward as the schools of our country suddenly had Federal Funds, they rushed to buy all the books and gadgets that they had hungered for so long a time.

Encyclopedia Britannica was one of the companies that almost stood alone in having a very wide variety of products to re-label and fit the need of almost any new Federal Legislation. They actually had assembly lines for Federal money all done in one stop! Naturally, encyclopedias, or as they spelled them encyclopaedies, were the big-ticket item, but they also had 16 mm films. Filmstrips, multi-media modules, textbooks, study prints, overhead projection materials and even materials for *teaching machines.*

For many years the warehouse and shipping facilities could pack and ship more orders than the sales department could produce. But then, the bonanza of orders flooded in and the shipping department fell behind and soon there were some 60 thousand orders sitting in the warehouse. Now the customers began to phone the salesmen asking, "Where's my order? When will you ship? We do have deadlines to make. If it doesn't arrive in time we will lose Federal Funds."

That pressure for information on deliveries finally reached the Vice President of Marketing. He posted the following letter on the warehouse bulletin board alongside of the time clock:

TO ALL WAREHOUSE AND SHIPPING EMPLOYEES

Today I was advised that you now have in your department over 60 thousand orders that nave NOT been shipped. Each day that list is growing longer!

Next Monday I will visit your facilities, and if those orders are not shipped, I will clean house. FIRE ALL OF YOU and hire people who CAN get the job done!

Sincerely,

Vice President of Marketing

The following Monday the Vice President did visit the warehouse and all those 60 thousand orders WERE GONE! The Shipping Department was working on the order that had come in the previous Friday!

The Vice President was so very pleased and impressed with his power to get the job done that he posted the following letter:

TO ALL WAREHOUSE AND SHIPPING EMPLOYEES:

It gives me great pleasure to advise you that we are now caught up. Our backlog problem is gone. It proves once again that when all of us are working together, we can GET THE JOB DONE!

As of the first of the month, EVERYONE will receive a twenty-five cents per hour increase in base pay! The main office and its management are proud of the job all of you have accomplished this past week!

Sincerely,

Vice President, Marketing

And now the **mystery** of such a generous management! What the Vice President of Marketing didn't know was that one of the lowly paid order fillers had fed the 60 thousand orders into the paper shredder. He didn't want to lose his job! The company never did discover who took care of the back order problem.

The Order was Too Large

Back in the early 20's when automobiles began to flow out of Detroit's auto plants, no one envisioned the concept "service station." Gasoline was contained in large metal containers mounted on wheels. The hand pump on top would fill a one-gallon can that had a spout. Believe it or not, one gallon at a time would be poured into the car's gas tank. Another believe it or not— the small town grocery stores sold gasoline. It was the main source for those who owned an automobile.

My dad went to work for the S. F. Bowser Pump Company, Fort Wayne, Indiana. His starting territory was Illinois, Wisconsin, Iowa, Missouri and Nebraska. He would take a train to the towns, hire a horse and wagon, and call on the people in the area who owned a car. In the beginning, it was believed that each owner would have his own tank and pump.

S.F. Bowser invented and patented a system where a large (at that time) 500 or 1000-gallon tank could be buried in the ground. Bowser's pump would draw the gasoline out of the ground and deliver it to the car in precise measured gallons. It was considered an almost unbelievable patent.

Dad had a lot of freedom and an easy-to-use expense account. Even though those were prohibition days, it was easy to find drink. In less than a year, he had a problem. From time to time he would check himself into a sanitarium to dry out. One time while working Elgin, Illinois, he found himself in a typical sanitarium. In the next bed was a man named Herman who had the same bottle problem. Usually the first day or two no one talked. They felt too miserable to do so. When they finally got to talking, each found the other interesting. They both were characters. Herman owned the largest coal and ice business in Elgin, and he found dad's job highly unusual and unique. He asked, "Jim, do you really believe there is a future to cars and gasoline?"

Dad reeled off all the statistics on how many cars had already been manufactured and what the future would hold.

When they left the sanitarium, the two men put two 50-gallon drums of gas on a horse-drawn wagon and went out on a Sunday afternoon to the dirt road that led from Chicago to Elgin. Concrete highways did not exist at the time. In a few hours they sold out using that one gallon can with a spout.

On the strength of that experience, Bunge bought all the corners of main roads leading in and out of Elgin. By delivering coal and ice to all the local farmers over many years, he knew them and they knew him. He made out contracts and offered to give each farmer a free tank and pump if he would sign a ten-year lease for gasoline. Herman signed up 1450 farmers.

When my dad sent in the order to Fort Wayne, old man Bowser got on a train to go to Elgin. His intent? To fire Jim Shannon. Most of the company employees knew the problem he had with drink. Elgin's population was twenty-one hundred at the time and to imagine in your wildest dreams that a town of that size could request a 1450 tank and pumps was ridiculous. Shannon must be on another spree!

But the order was legitimate, and instead of getting fired he got a raise. CEO's can quickly change their minds about drink, especially when the orders are big.

The Fisk Letters

The following letters are not duplicates of the original letters, but they are factual and as exact as memory can produce:

President
Fisk Rubber Company
Jeannette, Pennsylvania

Dear Sir:

I want to personally thank you for the wonderful opportunity you have given my husband, Bob. He has only worked for your company less than a year and yesterday he received his bonus check for $125 thousand.

It is a dream come true to find my husband working for a company that is so generous to its new employees.

Gratefully yours,
Nancy O. Hudson

This return letter was sent airmail Special Delivery:

Nancy O. Hudson
Portland, Oregon

Dear Mrs. Hudson,

Received your letter this morning. I am flying out to the West Coast this afternoon. Please do not deposit that check. There must be some mistake.

We tried to reach you by phone this morning. I hope we can meet and talk when I get to Portland.

Sincerely,
President, Fisk Tire & Rubber

The story behind these two letters? It happened back in the early fifties. The Fisk Rubber Company over-produced and shipped five million dollars worth of tires to the West Coast. When this happens in the rubber industry, the tire company involved would have someone slice off one of the letters of the company's name, in the case F I S K. What's left is I S K and this is a blemish. That made the tires flawed and the industry procedure was to unload them at 50 percent discount. That $5 million dollars at wholesale prices was now only two and a half million.

The West Coast had a young wheeler-dealer type of manager. He called in all of his West Coast sales force and said, "Let's not make these tires 'seconds.' Let's make this a special 25 percent discount!"

Instead of collecting two and a half million, we will collect three and three quarters million. If we do this, I think we can sell them quickly and we will split the one and a quarter million between the ten of us. That's $125,000 each! What a *BONUS!*

The Fisk president was frustrated. No one actually stole from the company. Their orders were to sell the lot for two and a half million and the tires were sold for three quarters million. Annoyed, embarrassed, all Fisk could do was fire all of them.

With a bonus of $125,000, no one cared.

Story Telling Can Be Dangerous

Sales people come in all sizes, kinds, and types: tall, short, thin, fat, handsome, and homely. On and on. A needed ingredient in each person is the ability to meet strangers easily, to fit in. To laugh, to make others laugh, is truly one of life's joys. This skill is a common talent in most salesmen. Telling stories is a daily routine. But at times there are some that would be better untold. The symbol of the three monkeys—hear no evil, see no evil, speak no evil—should be heeded.

That first day at a new company for any new salesperson brings stress, and a discomfort that is far from easy to endure. Initial impressions are made; some lasting a lifetime. A new recruit has a spotlight on him and he knows it. When possible, all new salesmen are hired prior to the company's national sales meeting. New products are introduced, old ones get glamour treatments. Policies and problems are rehashed. These sessions are programmed for sales training. All are encouraged to sit at different tables at each meal. Exchanges of ideas, problems and techniques are informally made. It is very worthwhile for the new and old employees to gain insights into each others' abilities. Stories are swapped. The new man told this one at breakfast.

An older couple was sitting down to lunch. The wife said, "What in the world is wrong with you, Henry? You have a suppository in your ear." Henry replied, "Thank you, Ellie. Now I know where my hearing aid is." All laughed. Later that day he noticed one of the men at his breakfast table was wearing a hearing aid.

The first monkey had has hands over his ears.

At the noon meal one of the men at his table said, "Hope all of you won't mind, I've always said grace before eating."

Naturally, all said, "Fine." When he finished praying, the new man told them that he recently heard an Irish blessing that was funny. "Thank you, Lord, for those who love us. May they always love us. For those who don't love us, please, Lord, turn their ankles so we will know them by their limping."

Most of the men chuckled. At an afternoon session, the storyteller noticed that the man who said grace had had a slight stroke and was limping a bit.

The second monkey had his hands over his eyes.

The evening sales session is usually a banquet. Cocktails before and wine with the meal. Supposedly it is fun time, but most people are guarded and careful. All are being observed. At the end of the meal the VP of sales will bring up to the main table and introduce to all, the new people who have come aboard. The new man was expected to tell a funny story. And he did. "The NBC Network ran an ad in the *Wall Street Journal*. They were looking for a new face and a new voice for national TV. Radio City, New York, was listed as the address for personal interviews. This man reading the ad went to Radio City. Going up to the information desk, he asked, "Wh-wh-where's the pp-personnel off-off-office?" He was told it was on the 40th floor. Up he went. Just a short time later down he came a dejected, sad, and sorrowful figure. The man at the desk being a kindly soul asked, "How did you do?"

"Oh-oh-oh, it's the s-s-same o-o-old p-pproblem. They don't hire Catholics." The one hundred man audience exploded. Loud roaring, belly laughs! One salesman bounced up and down on his chair, almost falling off. He was hysterical.

"The story is OK, but not that good. The new man was mystified.

Later he had a very embarrassing time. The VP sitting next to him at the main table was a gruff, cranky boss, universally disliked. Under stress or anger he had a severe speech impediment. He stuttered to complete incomprehensibility. All one hundred salesmen thought the new man had a lot of gall to take a shot at the VP when he had just come aboard. But he didn't know!

The third monkey had his hands over his mouth.

Poor Products

POOR PRODUCTS

There are few of us who will recognize, much less appreciate, the unbelievable set of circumstances that can or might plague a particular sale. The problems are endless:

1. Wrong size, shape, color and total number of a product will be shipped.

2. Trucks run off the highway and the product is destroyed.

3. Billing departments can type the wrong total on an invoice.

4. Competition will sell below cost. Your order will be returned.

5. Murphy's Law sums it up. "Whatever can go wrong will go wrong."

No Freeze-and It Didn't

The Korean War was the first time that the average American did not want to trade *butter for bullets*. That expression was common during those war years. The words meant that even though there was a war going on, and American soldiers were dying by the hundreds, no citizens wanted to change their life style. Rationing did not exist. Everything could be purchased. Gasoline and cars, meat and sugar, you name it. Everything you wanted was there, except permanent anti-freeze and industrial alcohol.

Prestone is the trade name for ethylene glycol. It had national recognition, and only limited amounts were available, not enough to satisfy even half the demand. American ingenuity came to the surface and a product came to the market to meet the demand for permanent anti-freeze. It was called *No-Freeze*. The fact that a car owner had to use this product in a different fashion than Prestone did not hinder the salesmen who pitched it.

Prestone could be added to the water in the car's cooling system and the motorist continued to add until the testing gauge showed the system could withstand twenty to thirty degrees below zero. *No-Freeze* could *not* be added to water. The cooling system had to be completely drained. This meant the motorist used more gallons of *No-Freeze*, but it was considerably cheaper.

A medium-sized automobile supply wholesaler got the franchise for the Chicago area. The contract had two important clauses. Full truckloads meant 600 cases. That was the minimum size order. The second was a certified check for each and every shipment. Interstate Distributing was the name of the company, and they had six fairly young salesmen. All were WWII veterans and were aggressive, ambitious, and hungry.

They sold between three and four full truckloads each week. They did this for over five weeks. Everyone was please and happy with the additional income. Then problems developed. No, not problems. Catastrophe struck! *No-Freeze* was not what everyone thought it to be. Basically, it was kerosene, only a bit more refined with a masking agent added to it to hide the recognizable odor of kerosene. The normal market for this product was bug sprays. All petroleum products have the ability to hold heat. Tests showed that *No Freeze* at times hit 400 degrees. Such a temperature could melt solder in the radiator. The other characteristic of that created this catastrophe was the fact that it could weaken, and at times melt, the rubber hoses in the cooling system. *No-Freeze* would then spray all over the engine and a fire would start. If the car happened to have neoprene hoses, *No-Freeze* did not affect the system. The Interstate group wished that neoprene was the only type of radiator hoses in all cars, but that wasn't so. Car fires occurred far too often.

One of Interstate's salesmen worked the south side of Chicago. He called on a black man named Walter Seames who owned a Standard Oil Station at Sixth & Michigan. Walter Seames had just returned from a car trip to visit his mother in rural Texas. The salesman walked in the door and

Walter pulled out gun that seemed to be a foot long. It looked like a cannon. His words were, "White boy, get your ass out of here before I blow your brains out." The salesman fled. Later he learned that when Walter Seames drove home to Texas to see his mother, his car caught fire and burned to the ground. This all happened on a lonely isolated back road in Texas. He walked and walked. Could you blame Walter for his violent anger?

The moral to this sales tale? Every salesman should *know everything* there is to know about the product he sells.

The Bristles Melted

As new products are developed, unusual techniques and different materials can bring excitement and sparkle to a salesman's daily life.

Paintbrushes with nylon bristles were introduced to the United States market. The old-fashioned brushes had always been made from pig bristles. Only China had both the pigs and the severe winter weather to make the pigs grow very long bristles. When demand for brushes increased, naturally the price of paintbrushes grew impossibly expensive.

Nylon, as a trade name, received immediate recognition and the price was almost 50 percent cheaper than pig bristles. The men went out and wrote orders. Large orders. Opened new accounts. The future looked great. No clouds on the horizon. Then catastrophe hit.

The brushes were never intended to be used in anything but water-based paint. The literature on the packaging did *not* mention that fact. When used in an oil-based paint, the kind that is thinned by turpentine or paint thinners, the nylon bristles disappeared. What do you say to a customer who returns to the store with a paintbrush handle? The bristles had melted and became part of the paint.

Most of our world enjoys thinking that we control, in some way, our destiny. A salesman's chances to do so are quite slim. The customers and the stores did get their money returned. Eventually, Dupont did produce a bristle that did not melt from petroleum based paint thinner.

*Car*nauba Wax for Cars

Selling can be fun, especially when a particular idea or program harms no one. Most of us feel that when one individual cheats another, inside the sharpies mind is the recognition that he is a thief. *Sell the sizzle not the steak* has been a central theme for years on end. Try to bring a sparkle, a joy, an interesting concept is always a sales team's goal. Romancing wax for a car isn't easy, but it did happen one day.

So many things in our lives are similar, if not identical. Wax is wax. You rub it on and rub it off. The car shines; you feel good. The fact that a shiny car brings joy to the owner is a strange concept when you think about it seriously. A small auto supplies dealer in a suburb outside Chicago came up with a clever idea. All car wax products at the time sold for $1.00 a bottle or can. This company wanted to sell their product for $2.00. A reason for the price change had to be apparent to the customer. One of the ingredients carnuba7 is a wax-like substance that some insects deposit on the leaves of certain bushes in West Africa. A bottle is a bottle. Theirs was not different. But the company attached a little 2" x 2" card with a red ribbon to the product telling the *car* nauba story

The card described the patience and time it took for natives to scrape the thin coating off the plant leaves, collect it in huge cases, carry it to seaport towns, and ship it to America. Was it any wonder that Carnauba wax costs more? Two dollars was a bargain!

Strange Names

Some products' names indicate their creators walk a very thin line. The name is not illegal. It does no harm. But it also does no good. The product actually does nothing. More than likely it has a good solid advertising program. Coupled with that ad budget will be an aggressive sales team that will be highly motivated by bonuses, special perks, or awards. Motovim was such a product. Examine the name itself *Motovim*—Motors and Vitamins. Imagine vitamins that help what's wrong with a motor. Some of the key phrases are—Doctors of motors recommend Motovim. The concept of doctor plus vitamins made it sell. Those are buzzwords in advertising.

For most oil additives, prices vary from $2.50 to $7.95 a quart,. Some of us are not only convinced but sincerely believe if something costs more its got to be worth more. The right names plus advertising know-how is a success formula to generate sales.

U.S. Royal Masters

Salesmen are told and retold by management and business schools alike, "*Know your product*. Know all about it. Be as knowledgeable as possible about all phases of what you sell. Sometimes that advice is desirable and at times it's not. Case in point:

The United States Rubber Company produced US Royal tires. The top of their line was the US Royal Master. It was heavily advertised and was original equipment on the top Cadillacs. Naturally, their advertising department took advantage of being in the Cadillac image. High-priced quality is the theme of most ads.

From time to time, the company ran ads that accented the idea that the Royal Master *digs* in when it turns a comer. The strange part of that advertising statement was that we are led to believe that rubber can *dig in*. Dig into concrete? Another problem with Royal Masters was the tread. The part of the tire that meets the road was narrower than the average tire. The advertising department takes the weakest characteristics and makes them into a positive feature. The less tread on the concrete the less surface to stop the car.

If the salesman knew the truth, would it be easier or more difficult to sell Royal Masters?

Letters A and B

Salesmen have more than their share of problems. Can anyone imagine the turmoil caused by the letters *A* and *B*?

In the early 30's the Old Ben Coal Company had its corporate office on the sixteenth floor of the Continental Illinois Savings Bank in downtown Chicago. This corporation had one product with most of its mines in Southern Illinois and a few in Kentucky. The Board of Directors was made up of old line Chicago First Families who for the most part lived in the Lake Forest area. Even though this was the depths of the Great Depression, the reality never touched the rich and the powerful from the right families.

A mail boy has all kinds of letters go through his hands. Most of them were invoices expecting someone to pay the company, or the company sends checks out to pay for products or services received. A dull, drab and dreary job for the most part, but every so often a letter going out or one coming in can get attention. More than that, some can be so disturbing that it makes one want to react, to do something about the wrong one sees.

The purchasing agent had been buying lumber from several companies and constantly pitted one supplier against the other to get a cheaper price. Most of this lumber was big, heavy beams to shore up the overheads in the mines. Because of a long period of mine disasters, it became necessary to have state inspectors check out the mines for safety.

One of the necessary, if not obligatory, rules for mine safety was that only grade A lumber would ever be used. Usually after fatal accidents, the rule was obeyed faithfully. But time weakens memories, and after a brief period the purchasing agent started pushing for cheaper prices, and class B lumber began to make its way into the mines.

Once in a while a lumber company hired a new employee who would send Old Ben an invoice for class B lumber. The purchasing agent would send a scathing letter back to the lumber supplier and demand a new invoice without the B label. It was done. This type of activity was common not rare.

The purchasing agent did not personally gain anything financially by this action. But he did curry favor with the bosses, those who reaped the benefit of cheaper B lumber, even though it might increase accidents.

The bosses only worry about the bottom line.

The Letters E and F

The Minnesota Mining and Manufacturing Company of St. Paul, Minnesota is a United States conglomerate that grew from 125 employees in WWI to such size that over 6,000 employees served in WW II.

The two men who ran 3M, Bush and McKnight, were hard and merciless taskmasters. Modern public relations departments work overtime to brighten the CEO's image and much of the past is forgotten, maybe *taped over* is a better phrase in this case.

Whenever Bush and McKnight would go to the Chicago office, all employees were forewarned at least twenty-four hours in advance. All were expected to wear their Sunday best and clear off their desks to show that every detail had been handled. No smiling or laughter was permitted. The dour Scots seem to believe that a happy, cheerful face goes hand in hand with laziness, indolence and lack of production. They were hard, mean skinflints and brooked no resistance. Whenever a serious error was committed, and any company doing millions and millions of volume will have mistakes, the blame must be placed on some one person. The label of serious was assigned according to the dollars lost by the mistake.

In 1941 Pullman Standard Car saw the war approaching and decided to completely refurbish their Pullman Cars, the sleepers. This meant painting and varnishing in great volume, and they gave3M an order for 50 thousand rolls of masking tape. An order this size happens once in a lifetime. The salesman who worked the area went to Pullman that same day. The following day his sales manager went to Pullman with him to thank the purchasing agent personally. Three days later, the V.P. of tape production arrived in Chicago and he too checked to make certain the delivery schedule was on time. All this was to show that the entire 3M organization was alert to the 50 thousand roll order.

But all was not well. Masking tape for painting is labeled *MF*. It is made with an adhesive that is easily removed when the paint or varnish dries. Masking tape for electrical use is marked *ME*. The adhesive used is of a permanent compound. Once in place it stays.

The order from Pullman specified *ME,* although everyone at 3M knew it was to be used for painting only. Fifty thousand rolls of electrical tape, *ME*, were shipped and Pullman used them all. When the painters tried to remove the tape, the wood veneer inside the cars pulled off. The cars were ruined. Pullman sued!

Now 3M had a problem. Who should receive blame? Bush and McKnight would learn of this serious mistake for sure. The salesman involved had started at 3M as a young man and was well liked. No one would blame him. His sales manager had family connections with the management and was untouchable. The vice president of production was far too powerful to be accused.

The girl who typed the order the way it was given to her was fired! That's right. Fired! Just like that. Rules are rules and a serious mistake demands that someone be fired. When the secretary left she wrote on her desk: 3M = A Mean, Miserable, Malicious Company!

Still one more example of the rocky road a salesman travels; the difference between E & F killed his bonus.

Successes

SUCCESSES

What Price Success

After World War II thirteen million men returned to civilian life. Each had approximately the same dream: marry your sweetheart, raise a family, get a car, a house in suburbia, go after the good life! This salesman married his sweetheart from seventh grade. "Vatican Roulette" didn't work, and eleven kids showed up in twelve years.

Being healthy, happy and hungry, he found he needed two jobs to support this larger brood. The first job was with the Clorox Corporation. He made daily calls on specific warehouses in the Chicago area. Those giant complexes fed the shelves of their particular chain. He would arrive at 6:00 A.M. to discover how many cases had been sent out that previous 24 hours. His job was over at 2:00 P.M.

The second sales position was with a South Bend Indiana brewery. The hours were from 3:00 P.M. till 1:00 A.M. and included as always the bars and liquor stores in a section of Cook County. For almost two years, all was well. He paid the bills, the babies kept coming, but he had little to worry about.

But summer sales contests created havoc. This hard working, hungry salesman drove hard to win the Clorox Sales Award and came in second at the company.

The National Sales Management Magazine ran articles with pictures of more than forty sales organizations. His name and picture appeared twice.

Clorox took the man to court. They wanted their pay and bonuses for the year to be repaid. The salesman with his wife and six kids, at the time, showed up before the judge. The trial was short when the judges turned to the Clorox legal team and asked, "Do you really want to sue this family?"

Moral: What do corporations want from their salesman, orders or subservience?

Listen Well

Salesmen have a worldwide image of being "gabby". The words spew out in a never-ending flow. But the wise ones, who have learned through hard experience, discover it pays to be a good listener, as well as being a good talker.

A classic example is my old boyhood friend named Al Ferguson. He was a highly experienced, successful salesman. Heavy industrial equipment and power tools had been his life's work. Al moved from one major company to another. A rule he lived by was that if the present sales job had hit its peak in volume or commissions, he would move on. He would never take a lateral move. Always up!

On a night like so many others, Al sat at bar of a major hotel in Detroit. The day had been successful. The man sitting next to him opened up the conversation with the usual; "Did you have a good day?"

After exchanging names of company, hometown, kids, they finally got down to the day's sales efforts. Ferguson was not only a fine talker, but he was a better listener. He had learned early in his sales life that if you think the man you are talking to is dull, it's your fault. You have not asked the right questions. Each of us has a story to tell with unique experiences and backgrounds.

The salesman next to Al at the bar was in the insurance field. His company covered liabilities and problems of major utilities and transportation. That day his manager had sent him to the home office of a railroad. He was to inform the railroad president that the premiums would rise 400 percent and that the first $10 thousand of each claim would be the railroad's responsibilities.

The catastrophic railroad problem was in the hauling of newsprint from Canadian paper mills to major United States newspapers. The weight of these rolls of paper was unbelievable. The freight cars had wooden floors, or if metal, the thickness was only sufficient for normal weights, not for newsprint. Freight cars are not cushioned and even if the jolts are light as it travels, the constant repetition eventually creates a crack, a split, and water splashes in on the newsprint rolls. These rolls of paper expand and their increased weight and volume literally rips freight cars apart. The power is awesome.

Hundreds of freight cars hauled thousands of rolls of newsprint. The volume of both freight cars and newsprint being destroyed continued to mount. The cost of this catastrophe was phenomenal. The misfortune affected all the newspaper companies. Newsprint is an absolute necessity to maintain publication schedules. The paper mill lost the value of the paper. The railroad freight cars were being destroyed. Both the railroads and the paper mills were in serious financial trouble. An answer was needed

Next morning, Al went to the president of the railroad and said he would return with a policy at the old rate if the company would allow the paper mills to refurbish specific cars to carry their rolls. His next trip was to an insurance firm that would take the business if the railroad would be accident free. A commission arrangement was made. Detroit Steel which produced and manufactured tank steel used in World War II made a financial arrangement with the paper mills.

This last agreement, and probably the most difficult to accomplish, was to have the paper mills pay for the installation of the steel in the railroad freight cars. The mills had the greatest financial losses when the rolls were destroyed and the huge, swollen newsprint had to be dumped somewhere. Not an easy fix. The mills okayed the venture; they had the most to gain. The railroad, the insurance company, Detroit Steel and finally the paper mills were all happy with the solution.

Al was a good listener. He was a dreamer and a schemer along with being determined and persistent. This is a classic case of what "Good Listening" can accomplish. Plus Al did have an *artist's flair* for fine salesmanship.

A Success Story

The success story of Ray Kroc of McDonald hamburger fame is almost unbelievable. He was the dreamer, the schemer, blessed with determination and persistence. He asked questions and did listen. He acted cautiously and wisely. The story of Ray Kroc's life is one to admire and emulate.

But not all of it!

Oak Park River Forest High School is in Chicago's suburban west side. It has a solid middle-income population, but there are some palatial homes, too. The student body is representative of a cross-section of the United States. Ray Kroc at the end of his sophomore year was expelled. His listless, careless, inattentive attitude infuriated the counseling staff. So he was booted out. Their considered opinion was that he was a complete ne'r-do-well and would never amount to much.

How wrong they were! Kroc got a sales job peddling ice cream mixers for a company that was located in Indianapolis, Indiana. The company's best customers were the owners of hamburger stands that existed on the outskirts of our nations villages. Theses stands were small, but they did not have indoor seating. When the cold weather came, most of these places of business either closed or went bankrupt. The ice cream machines bought on credit were never paid for.

Ray Kroc traveled the nation selling his ice cream mixers. Being astute, he noticed that McDonalds of California was well run, successful, and paid its bills.

This fabulous story should not be told in these few words. Kroc watched, Kroc listened, and Kroc learned! He asked for permission to open a duplicate stand near by. The explosion of McDonald hamburger outlets erupted! Wherever there are people the world over, they can find the golden arches of McDonalds. Who knows why!

It seems an ingredient to the mental makeup of an outstanding sales personality is a "chip on the shoulder" attitude. These men put in the extra effort to be successful. Maybe Ray Kroc being expelled from high school gave him a hidden drive.

Ask for the Order

One of the rules of selling that is constantly stressed by sales organizations is always remember to *"Ask for the order."* There must be hundreds of ways to ask.

"Do you want to charge it"?
"When should we deliver?"
"Do you want quarts or gallons?
"Which color do you prefer?"
"How many do you want? "
"Is this the size you want?"

On and on. This story is about a highly unusual way to ask for the order.

During the late 60's a division of Singer, the S.V.E. Company sold film strips to all the schools in the United States. One saleman's territory was Indiana. East Chicago, Indiana is a steel mill and a gasoline refinery center for the Midwest. The stench, the smog, the lack of trees and vegetation make the area a highly unpleasant place to live and work. Naturally, the area is peopled by many poorly educated, low-income families usually immigrants to the United States.

Under the rules developed by the legislature in Washington, D.C., educational departments like East Chicago, Indiana were given extra funds to purchase materials. A friendly, rough-spoken man was in charge of the audio/visual center there. Because of the extensive funds available to him, he was wined and dined by every educational representative who had any products that might fall under the audio/visual label. He was an affable, likable man who enjoyed eating and was a bit on the "chunky" side. At lunch he would take a drink or two. S.V.E. being a tight-fisted, stingy, conservative organization, the managers constantly harangued their sales force regarding expenses. Lunches were frowned upon; a salesman was absolutely required to deliver a signed order to accompany a luncheon check receipt.

The S.V.E. salesman who worked East Chicago enjoyed the audio/visual director's companionship. Maybe twice a year the two of them would go to Phil Schmidt's, a local restaurant that was famous for its fish and chicken. A Manhattan straight up with cherry juice, no less, was the first order. At times this client would have two, but never more. The S.V.E. salesman did receive some business from the account but not enough, as far as his home office management was concerned, to justify lunches. S.V.E. continued nagging the salesman that the audio/visual director was a *"sponge "* and would continue to work him for lunch and drinks. At this time, East Chicago schools were improving their inventory and requested all new products be brought in for evaluations.

One day, the salesman made his usual bi-yearly call with lunch, cherry juice Manhattans, the whole scene. One more time, he discussed new products. The audio/visual director once again showed interest, but did not buy. The S.V.E. man said, "Look, I like you. I like coming here. We always have a good time when we get together. You don't have to con me about what you will buy. I do receive some business from you, but not that much. So either shit or get off the pot."

The director kind of ruffled up a bit and said, "That's no way to talk to a customer. What the hell are you talking about?"

The salesman answered, "Sorry, but S.V.E. nags me that you've been talking about a big order for years, and it never happens."

The next question from the audio/visual director was, "How much is your whole catalog worth?"

The answer was $9,000.

The customer said, "Send it!"

When the order came into the Chicago office, believe it or not, the sales manager was annoyed. The audio/visual director *bought* when everyone said that he never would. Two weeks later, the president asked how the order was obtained.

"Shit or get off the pot!" the salesman said.

"That's no way to talk," the president barked.

Obviously it isn't, but it worked!

A Color Can Do It

The Deep Rock Oil Corporation chief executive officer was Bernard J. Majewski, nicknamed *"Barney."* He was a very colorful, aggressive, hard-driving boss. He was one of those rare individuals who not only survived, but actually thrived on a minimum of sleep. Most nights it was only three or four hours. By starting his day early, he would at times complete an eight-hour day of work before the average man started.

Barney was proud of his humble beginnings. Born and raised on the northwest side of Chicago, which is the second largest Polish settlement in the world, he had many stories about his humble beginning. One particular story, quite raunchy but still believable, had to do with Saturday night baths. The flat he lived in did not have a bathtub. A huge galvanized, round tub was placed in the middle of the kitchen floor. His mother would fill it with water heated on the kitchen stove. Barney was the youngest, so he was the last to use the tub. When asked if the water was dirty, he would answer, "Not too bad, but I never got used to the smell of urine." His observation points out what a character Barney was.

Almost every oil company spends considerable time and money on its public image, the colors used to further identification. Some are green and white; others red, white and blue; blue and white, and on and on. Deep Rock called in a color consultant who conducted lengthy surveys in both urban and rural markets. Deep Rock was advised their best color combination would be a strong yellow and a medium blue. Again, a very clever salesman pushed for this combination. Barney Majewski liked the combination; it happened to be the colors of the Polish National Flag.

Corporate Integrity

General Tire had a salesman named Bob Murphy. He was a very warm, friendly and likeable guy. After just a few minutes in his presence, a person felt like he knew Murphy all of his life. He could drink and tell stories, laugh and sing almost without end. He would disappear for a week at a time doing just that. His favorite bars would answer the phone, "Miller's Garage" or O'Brien's Automotive" to help him cover his tracks with the home office. When he went after a competitor's best account, he almost always got it. His Irish charm and good humor were infectious, and few resisted his sales pitch.

General Tire did not have a strong distributor in the Seattle or Portland areas. Firestone had a solid dealer who had stores in both cities. Murphy was sent out to try to get the dealer to switch to General.

Over the years, Murphy had developed a reputation with the accounting department at General as being a wild spender. Most of their sales force kept their entertainment budget to a maximum of $100 a given week. Most weeks were far less. But not Bob Murphy. He had become such a thorn in the side that the problems with Murphy went all the way up to W. E. O'Neill, the C.E.O., the president and major stockholder of General Tire.

The first night on the West Coast, Murphy took the dealer to dinner. The dealer was a big spender too, but with a purpose. At restaurants he would send bottles of champagne over to tables where some of his customers were sitting. At the end of the evening, the tab came to more than $500 and Murphy grabbed the check. When his expense account hit the office, he got a phone call and was asked if it was true that there were only two for dinner!

Bob said "Yes" and went on to explain the habits of the tire dealer who sent champagne to customers' tables. They angrily asked Bob why he didn't let the dealer pick up the bill. Murphy's answer was, "I didn't want to look cheap."

All this conversation and the dinner receipts were fed into President O's hands and he snorted "Fire him!"

By this time, Murphy and the tire dealer were bosom buddies. It took two or three days for General tires home office to find Murphy. The two got lost somewhere. Murphy was fired over the phone. Murphy's answer stunned home office. He asked, "You're sure now. I'm fired?"

And again he was told, "There is no doubt about it. You're fired!"

Bob said, "Fine, I agree. I no longer sell General Tires, but what do I tell this new customer? I saw his books and between Seattle and Portland last year, he ordered six million dollars worth of tires."

Murphy was given a new contract, a Buick to drive instead of a Chevrolet, and a raise on the limits to his expense account. Success has its own rules!

Dollar Volume of an Order

Salesmen never can predict the size of an order. At times the anticipation can be both full of hope and despair. One time in Ohio, our salesman lived near Columbus, which is close to the geographical center of the state. This allowed him to call on almost 80 percent of the schools without staying overnight anywhere. At times it was necessary to get up quite early to get to the schools by 9:00 A.M. An assistant superintendent at Kettering, Ohio phoned him one day and said he had a good order and requested that he get there by 7:30 A.M. He needed to discuss a problem with part of it.

Our salesman was up at 4:30 A.M. to make certain to arrive by 7:30. Kettering is a very affluent suburb of Dayton and has an excellent school system. They met on time and our man received a purchase order for $250. Specific code numbers were needed to make certain that exact items would be shipped. That was cleared up in a few minutes. He folded the order and said something like that's great. "Where are the others?"

The assistant superintendent looked at him oddly and said, "What others? That's it." It was early and our salesman was off guard and said, "I got up at 4:30 A.M. to drive one hundred miles to make $18.75? I'm on a 7.5 percent commission and pay my own expenses."

The superintendent's feelings were ruffled and it took our man a few minutes to placate him. Customers are always right, but there are times when that fact is difficult to accept. Now here is the other end of the scenario.

Paul Briggs, the Cleveland Superintendent of Schools had a session at the White House with President Johnson. When the President found that the Cleveland Schools did not have visual aids in each building he was flabbergasted. He said, "Briggs, let me see what I can do." In a matter of minutes he said, "Here is $540 thousand for visual aids. But there is a hitch. The funds must be spent within a week."

Paul Briggs phoned his AV Director, Ms. Lenore Portias and told her the details. Mrs. Portias was new to Cleveland. She had transferred to that system from Kent State University. She knew very few people selling audiovisual materials. But she was familiar with Larry Leapley who worked for McGraw-Hill's 16mm film division. McGraw also made filmstrips. Portias requested a $2700 package for each of two hundred schools. Larry Leapley provided a filmstrip projector plus a collection of one hundred fifty filmstrips. He received the order over the phone without even driving to Cleveland.

Larry eventually became a National Sales Manager because of that order. Salesmen live with uncertainty. One never knows!

www.ingramcontent.com/pod-product-compliance
Lightning Source LLC
Chambersburg PA
CBHW030744180526
45163CB00003B/910